Making Furniture

John Trussell

Dryad Press Ltd, London

First published 1970 by B T Batsford Ltd

This edition published 1984

ISBN 0 8521 9591 5

Printed and bound
in Great Britain by
Butler & Tanner Ltd
Frome, Somerset
for the Publishers
Dryad Press Ltd
4 Fitzhardinge Street
London W1H 0AH

Contents

Acknowledgment

The author is pleased to acknowledge the help he has received in assembling the information in this book from the various firms who have assisted him, especially those mentioned by name in the text and to Ridley and Hoopers of Bury St Edmunds. He would like to apologise to firms producing similar products to those referred to who are not mentioned.

He is greatly indebted to Batsfords for the courtesy, help and advice received from Miss Thelma M. Nye who has managed to reduce everything to some semblance of order and see it through to publication. Also he would like to thank Mr B. M. Chester for reading and checking the proofs.

Introduction

This book is written for the express purpose of helping those who have acquired a basic knowledge of woodworking techniques and who now want to progress to designing and making their own furniture. It is not its purpose to provide ready made solutions for all problems or to offer completed designs but to present at least some of the possibilities and their advantages and disadvantages and leave it to the reader to choose his own answer. To this end the book is divided into several parts with the writing deliberately kept to a minimum to make reference easy.

The second part is intended as a guide to designing technique. It offers a method of approach to design which can be applied to any problem. By taking a simple example it shows how to get beyond preconceived ideas and find a new solution. It then applies the suggested method to a specific design problem.

The remainder of the parts provide readily accessible material to supplement the designer's own knowledge. He can select the joint which best suits his requirements, find the fitting that does just what he wants and the right finish to complete the job. He will be saved from making some mistakes and will be made aware of new possibilities. He will also be encouraged to tackle more advanced work than he might otherwise do.

It is hoped that it will provide a very welcome reference book for the amateur craftsman both at home and at school.

1 Timber

There are many different materials used in modern furniture manufacture, plastics, metal and cardboard, materials which, a few years ago, would not have been considered. These may provide articles of a functional nature but they lack the beauty and satisfaction which comes from using wood. This beauty remains throughout the life of the piece of furniture. As it ages it develops, through polishing and handling, a patina peculiar to wood. This book is primarily concerned with natural woods although various modern materials are introduced when appropriate.

The cabinet maker must not only know his wood, he must also be in sympathy with it. He must know its strength and its weakness and use it to its best advantage, asking it to do only those things for which it is best suited. He designs in such a way that the wood is favourably displayed not to show off his own clever construction. He will store a board having especially choice grain and colour until just the right job comes along. Rather like a sculptor working in wood lets it suggest the subject rather than the other way round.

The outstanding quality of wood is its great natural beauty. Words cannot describe the appearance of a polished walnut panel with all its gradations of colour. No one can improve on it, it just needs showing to advantage. Similarly an attractively figured oak board is complete in itself. But it takes a craftsman to find it, converting the tree in a particular way and selecting each board with great care. Even here the layman would miss the latent beauty. But the expert sees, beneath the rough sawn face, what the wood will be like when it has been cleaned up and polished. He knows from experience the transformation that will take place as he works on it, until with a final inspection he announces the job finished.

Nor are any two pieces of wood exactly the same, indeed it is common to find one end of a board quite different from the other. Some manufacturers use stain to reduce all the pieces to a uniform colour but the hand craftsman lets the wood speak for itself. Not all woods are equally attractive but possibly because they are cheaper and stable are kept for the hidden parts of furniture, the sides and bottoms of drawers for example.

If wood is to be used intelligently it is necessary to have some knowledge of the way it grows and how it behaves after it has been felled and converted for use. While the tree is growing it is full of sap and when it is felled and converted into boards it must be seasoned (dried out) before it is ready for use. This means reducing the moisture content to around 15 per cent. There are two stages in this process, in the first the 'free water' within the cells dries out and no change of shape takes place. In the second stage the cell walls themselves dry out and at this point shrinkage does occur. It would be disastrous if this movement were to happen after the piece of furniture was made.

Figure 1a shows the cross section of a tree with the sapwood unshaded and the heartwood shaded. A tree grows by adding a ring to its growth each year. This takes place just under the bark and the sap runs freely in this area. Thus the further you are from the heart the more moisture there is to dry out.

The position of two boards is illustrated by pairs of parallel lines on the first illustration. The top one is well away from the heart and the lower one passes through it. The top face of the first board will contain more moisture than the lower face and proportionally through it and so, as it dries out, the top will shrink more than the bottom causing it to warp. The direction of warp or curve is indicated by the arrows and is always away from the heart. The second board will remain flat although it will shrink in width and thickness as it dries out, see figures 1a and b.

Wood shrinks about its width and thickness but the length remains, for all practical purposes, unaltered. The shrinkage will continue until the wood has reached the same state of moisture content as the atmosphere in which it is placed. It can be reduced below this level by artificial means but it will then absorb moisture until a state of equilibrium is reached. Should the local conditions change, and this is happening all the time, the wood will react and expand or contract as the humidity goes up or down. This will continue throughout the life of the timber although the amount of movement becomes less as the timber gets older.

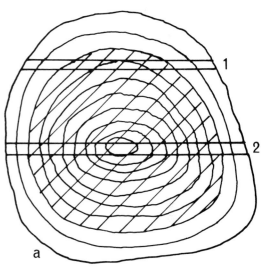

1a   Cross section of a tree trunk with sapwood unshaded and heartwood shaded area

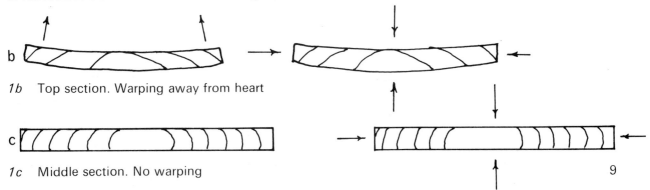

1b   Top section. Warping away from heart

1c   Middle section. No warping

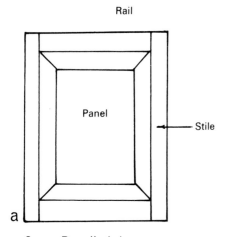

Rail

Panel

Stile

2 *a* Panelled door
  b Section showing
  panel held in groove

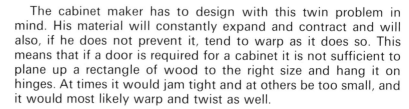

The cabinet maker has to design with this twin problem in mind. His material will constantly expand and contract and will also, if he does not prevent it, tend to warp as it does so. This means that if a door is required for a cabinet it is not sufficient to plane up a rectangle of wood to the right size and hang it on hinges. At times it would jam tight and at others be too small, and it would most likely warp and twist as well.

This problem is overcome by making a panelled door (see *2a* and *b*). The width of the rails and stiles is kept to a minimum and the panel is held unglued in a groove so that it can expand and contract but not warp. The door remains true and any alterations to its outside measurements are too small to be of importance. The method of securing table tops and other problems in this field are dealt with in Part 5.

Wood cells are long and narrow and bound loosely together. A chopper illustrates how easily the bond is broken. Figures *3a* and *b* show two seesaws. In the first the grain is running across the board and it would collapse as soon as it was used while the second would last as long as it was required.

This means that the grain must 'run round' a box if it is to have any strength, this is illustrated in figure *4a* and *b*. If a mistake is made, as could easily happen if one of the ends was square, it would only require a slight knock for it to shatter. *5a* and *b* show two handles, in (*a*) the shaping is brought down almost to a point which has such little strength that the corners would most likely fall off during making or while gluing. This has been corrected in (*b*) to produce a strong handle.

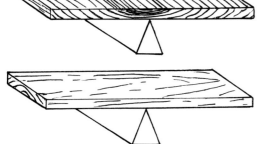

3 *a* Short grain seesaw
  b Long grain seesaw

4 *a* Grain running round a box
  b Grain running round a box

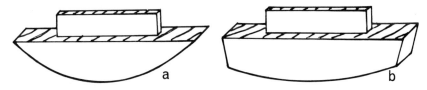

5 *a* Unsuccessful handle
  b Successful handle

By the same reasoning dovetails and tenons must have the grain running along them as in *6a* and *b*. If they were made with the grain running across they would have no strength at all. This is also apparent in the handles already referred to.

When the grain runs across or obliquely across a piece of wood then it is termed short grained as opposed to one where the grain runs straight down it. (*7a* and *b*.) Any deviation from the straight means a loss in strength. In order to achieve this maximum strength with a curved member like a chair leg a board is carefully chosen which has a matching curve to the grain. (*8*).

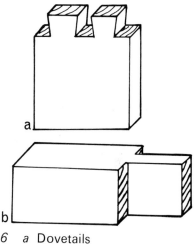

6 *a* Dovetails
  b Tenon

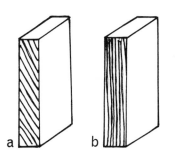

7 *a* Short grain
  b Long grain

8 Grain selected to run in same direction as shape of leg

9 Curved grain in chestnut showing how this curve can be utilised

11

A selection of timbers

Abura   Not a very interesting timber but suitable for hidden details; e.g. drawer sides, etc.

Afrormosia   A useful cabinet timber similar to teak.

Agba   Another rather colourless timber similar to Abura. Slight odour attached to it, unsuitable for food storage.

American Whitewood   Works cleanly, suitable for drawer sides.

Ash   The example in the photograph is olive ash. It can vary from this colour to near white.

Beech (Red)   The colour comes from steam seasoning. Very hard wearing, tough to work, uniform in colour, takes a good polish.

Beech (White)   Similar to the above, except in colour.

Cherry   An attractive wood with variety in colour and markings.

Chestnut   Similar to oak but without figuring, very attractive grain, useful cabinet wood.

Elm   Not always easy to obtain sound boards.

Freijo   A cabinet timber with a wide range of colours making matching difficult using random boards.

Mahogany (Brazil)   A very even-grained wood with consistent colour, mild working.

Mahogany (Honduras)   Traditional favourite with the cabinet maker.

Mahogany (Phillipines)   Covers quite a wide range of wood (*see note page 19*).

Mahogany (West Africa)   Similar to Honduras but lacks the quality.

Oak (Europe)   A lovely timber to work, finishes cleanly, polishes well.

Oak (Brown)   If obtainable, makes an attractive rich brown wood with oak characteristics.

Oak (Japan)   Needs careful sorting to exclude sap, samples vary greatly in quality, slightly pink cast.

Rosewood (India)   Turns nicely to make handles, expensive, polishes well.

Sapele   Attractive colour but inclined to be unstable in use.

Sycamore   Best quality white, used for bureau fitments, as a veneer for interior of cocktail cabinets.

Teak Rather a dull stable timber, very durable.

Utile Similar to Sapele but rather more stable.

Walnut (Europe) Difficult to obtain but well worth the effort. Polishes well, most attractive timber prized by cabinet makers.

Walnut (West Africa) Possible alternative to European variety.

Yew Soft wood, polishes well, fair number of natural defects, knots etc, which must be accepted.

1 *Afrormosia*

2 *American Whitewood*

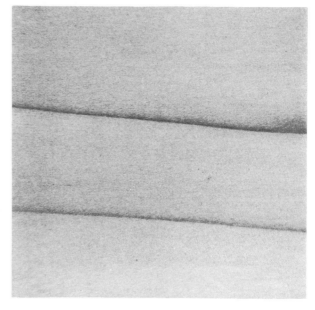

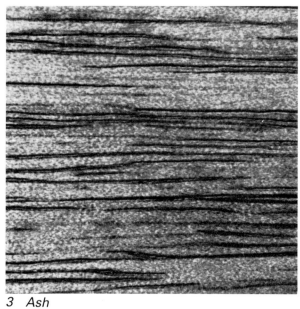

3 Ash

5 Chestnut

4 Beech (White)

6 Elm

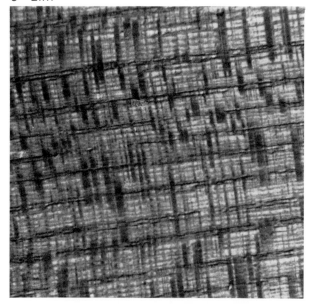

14

7 *Freijo*

9 *Mahogany (Honduras)*

8 *Mahogany (Brazil)*

10 *Mahogany (Phillipines)*

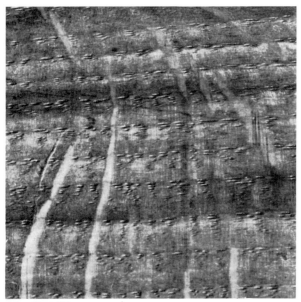

11 Oak (European)

12 Oak (Japan)

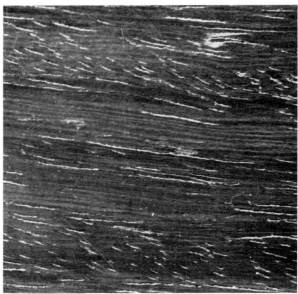

13 Rosewood

14 Sycamore

15 Cherry

17 Sapele

16 Utile

18 Yew

Timber and how it behaves

Movement of seasoned timber
- L Large
- M Medium
- S Small

Technical Note No. 38 revised 1982
Princes Risborough Laboratory
Aylesbury
Buckinghamshire HP17 9PX

Steam bending properties

Radius of curvature in inches		
Less than 6	Very Good	VG
15–25	Good	G
26–50	Moderate	M
51–75	Poor	P
Exceeding 75	Very Poor	VP

Technical Note No. 11, reprinted 1980
Princes Risborough Laboratory

Natural Durability

Very Durable	VD
Durable	D
Moderately Durable	MD
Not Durable	ND
Perishable	P

Technical Note No. 40, reprinted 1983
Princes Risborough Laboratory

Gradings used in the table of timbers

£12 to £15 a cube	A
£15 to £20 a cube	B
£20 to £40 a cube	C
Over £40 a cube	D

Supplied by William Mallinson & Sons
130 Hackney Road
London E2 7QR

Commonly used hardwoods

Wood	Country of origin	Price	Colour	Movement	Bending	Natural Durability
Abura	West Africa	A	Straw/Pink Brown	S	VP	ND
Afrormosia	West Africa	B/C	Brownish Yellow	S	M	VD
Agba	West Africa	A	Straw/Light Brown	S	M	D
American Whitewood	America	A/B	White/Greeny White	–	–	ND
Ash	Europe	A/B	White/Cream/Brown	M	VG	P
Beech Red	Europe	B/C	Pink Flecked	L	VG	P
Beech White	Europe	A/B	White Flecked	L	VG	P
Cherry	Europe	A/B	Yellow/Pink/Brown	M	VG	MD
Chestnut	Europe	B/C	Straw/Yellow/Brown	S	G	D
Elm	Europe	A/B	Grey/Brown	M	VG	ND
Freijo	Brazil	B	Dark/Light Brown	M	P	D
Mahogany	Brazil	B	Medium Red	S	M	D
Mahogany	Honduras	C	Pink/Dark Red Brown	M	R	D
*Mahogany	Phillipines	B	Rich Dark Red	S	P	MD to D
Mahogany	West Africa	B/C	Light/Dark Red Brown	VP	MR	MD
Oak	Europe	C/D	Yellow Brown	M	VG	D
Oak Brown	Europe	B/C	Rich Brown	M	–	–
Oak	Japan	C/D	Pink/Yellow Brown	M	VG	–
Rosewood	India	D	Dark Purple	S	–	VD
Sapele	West Africa	B/C	Red Brown	M	P	MD
Sycamore	Europe	A/B	White	M	VG	P
Teak	Burma	C/D	Yellow/Brown	S	M	VD
Utile	West Africa	B/C	Red Brown	S	M	D
Walnut	Europe	B/C	Grey/Dark Brown	M	VG	MD
Walnut	West Africa	B/C	Yellow Brown/Brown	–	M	MD
**Yew	Europe	B/C	Straw Pink/Red	–	G	D

*Phillipines Mahogany includes Red Lauan, Meranti and Seraya whose properties may vary.
**Yew is a soft wood which is used like a hardwood.

2 Design

Wood is essentially a beautiful material and if care is taken even the most difficult piece of timber can take on a smooth finish which will show off the infinite variety of markings which are naturally there. The range of wood available allows a great choice of colour and within the timber chosen or even the individual board there is continuous and subtle change which ensures that no two pieces will ever look exactly alike.

The designer with wood as his basic material has this tremendous advantage. His raw material is beautiful and attractive before he starts to do anything and nothing he can do can compete with this natural loveliness. His task, then, is to provide the means for displaying it.

No elaborate shapes are necessary to supply interest, this is there already, provided by the wood itself. All the designer has to do is to make the outline harmonise with the wood and its environment. The hanging book rack or display wants to 'belong' to the wall and not to stick out awkwardly.

He wants his shapes to be interesting and satisfying so that the eye travels easily around. For this purpose a curve is more pleasing than a straight line because a straight line is monotonous. A table top should not be left simply as a rectangle when a very slight curve would transform the shape.

A large amount of furniture is based on the rectangle. There are various formulae for working out certain rectangles which are said to be especially well proportioned. It is not necessary to know or use these formulae to achieve a satisfactory result. One thing that should be remembered is that a square or a near square is not a very happy solution. The eye tends to be 'unsettled' and gets worried in case it isn't exactly equal in length and height. A definite rectangle is much to be preferred.

The intending designer should study as much furniture as possible by going to the most reputable shops to see what is being made and by visits to the Design Centre and the Craft Centre. He should make copious sketches and measured drawings (a scale of $\frac{1}{8}$ in. to 1 in. is suitable). In this way he will become familiar with his subject and have a wealth of experience to draw upon.

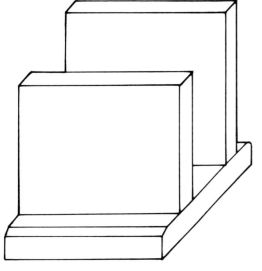

11 Basic book rack

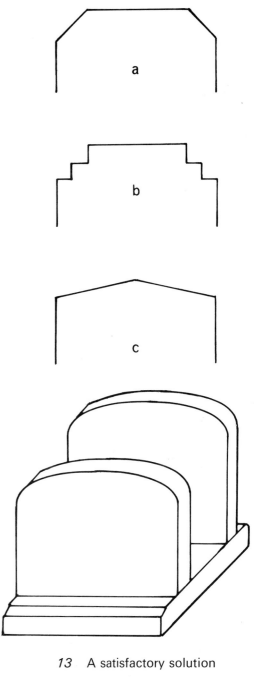

The problem

To attempt to lay down what is or is not good design seems dangerously arbitrary. A study of the subject merely confirms the view that good design is easily confused with current fashion which varies all too inconsistently. On the other hand there are certain points which can be taken up and illustrated which will help designers to think more clearly about the problems they are trying to solve.

There are two quite different questions which will arise. In one the designer has, within limits, a free hand in choosing a particular shape and in the other he finds that decisions which are outside his control fix the basic shape that he has to start with. There will also be combinations of both.

Look at a simple example of the free shape. Imagine you are designing a letter rack, the size is by no means critical provided the letters are firmly held and there is enough room. The point to be considered is the shape of the partitions. Figure *11* starts with a basic rack with the corners left square and then goes through a series of shapes starting with straight lines and finishing with curves. Figure *12a* is a possibility, it takes away the sharpness of the corner; *12b* is terrible and forces the eye to go up in jerks; *12c* is an improvement on *12a* because it joins the sides and top rather more smoothly; *12d* is similar to *12a* while *12e* is most offensive, the eye is shot off instead of moving smoothly round the corners; figure *13* does all that is required. It is still a simple shape, although made up of two different curves, and it acts as a complete link bridging the sides and also providing a little interest.

Other examples of this first type of problem are provided by a book end, a coffee table top, the end of a small hanging display cabinet, the end of a bookrack (this latter is dealt with in detail later on) and a table lamp. There are some limiting factors but broadly the designer is left to himself to find a shape satisfying both functionally and aesthetically.

13   A satisfactory solution

Assembling facts

Take a piece of paper and jot down all the questions that occur to you about the article you are designing.

> What is its function?
> What is it to hold and how many of them?
> What size are they, how heavy?
> Is it to stand on the floor or hang on the wall?
> Has it to fit in with any other furniture?
> Is it to withstand especially heavy wear?
> Is there a price ceiling?

These are just some of the questions that will occur and they will vary with different jobs. Once the list is complete then they should be answered. It is very likely that there will be two or even more answers to a number of the questions. For example, the books could be stored in a bookcase which stands on the floor or it could be secured to the wall. All these various solutions should be written down.

There will probably be certain points which allow no choice at all. Perhaps the article has to fit in with other furniture and it is felt that the same wood should be used. Taking the bookcase example again it could be that it is to be designed to hold a set of encyclopaedias and the internal dimensions are therefore fixed. Again it might have to fit into a recess between a wall and the chimney breast thus deciding the extreme sizes. These essentials should be shown very clearly on the information sheet.

Preliminary sketches

The designer now has in front of him the broad details on which he can set to work. He should make as many different sketches as he can and try to explore all the possibilities.

Imagine that the project is a magazine rack and he has been allowed a relatively free hand. He will find the answers to his various problems in the sections which follow this one. By consulting section twelve he finds that a magazine requires $13\frac{1}{2}$ in. by 11 in. of space. He then starts sketching and figure *14* shows the result of his work. He sees that the rack could stand

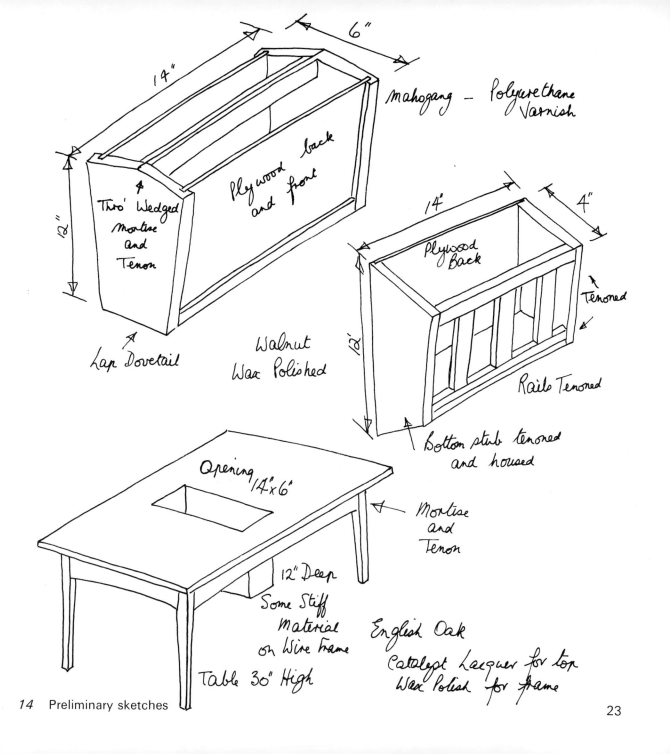

6"

14"

mahogany – Polyurethane Varnish

12"

Thro' Wedged Mortise and Tenon

Plywood back and front

Lap Dovetail

Walnut Wax Polished

14"

4"

Plywood Back

12'

Tenoned

Rails Tenoned

Bottom stub tenoned and housed

Opening 14"x 6"

Mortise and Tenon

12" Deep

Some Stiff Material on Wire Frame

Table 30" High

English Oak

Catalyst Lacquer for top Wax Polish for frame

14   Preliminary sketches

on a table or shelf, be fastened on the wall or be part of an actual table and the sketches illustrate these three ideas. They are freehand but roughly to scale so that they give a fair idea of what each example would look like.

To make sure that they can be made the drawings should have noted the joints which are intended to be used and section three will supply the answers. While he is doing this the designer should try to visualise himself gluing up the article and go through the motions in his mind just to see that it is feasible.

The sketches should include the wood and finish. Sections 1 and 11 will give all the help that is required here. The finish will be decided by the use to which the job is to be put. If the surface is to have a lot of handling and to resist damp and heat it would be wrong to use wax polish and one of the wood seals would be more suitable.

Exploring the chosen sketch

Choose the sketch that most nearly fulfils the requirements of the brief and draw it to scale. Do this a number of times varying the sizes this way and that. In figure *15* this technique has been applied to a coffee table. The height, length, leg and top shape and arrangement of stretcher rail have all been varied to see what effect they have on the appearance.

Figure *15a* shows four different table top shapes; in (*b*) the first table has parallel legs, the second has tapered ones, in the next the rail is curved and the last has a stretcher rail added; row (*c*) shows the effect of angling the legs and repeating the variations in the row above; (*d*) illustrates the same table but the stretcher rail is moved up and down. Notice how these changes affect the whole design as the rectangles formed between the rails and the stretcher rail and the floor alter in proportions; (*e*) gradually decreases the length of the top; (*f*) increases the height. These are only some of the changes that can be made; there are many more, e.g. the amount of overhang of the top, the dimensions of the top, the degree of slope of the legs, the dimensions of the legs, the arrangement of the underframing and so on and so on. All these variations will still be within the brief and the choosing of the right one will determine whether the final solution is a happy one or not.

15   Variations for coffee table ▶

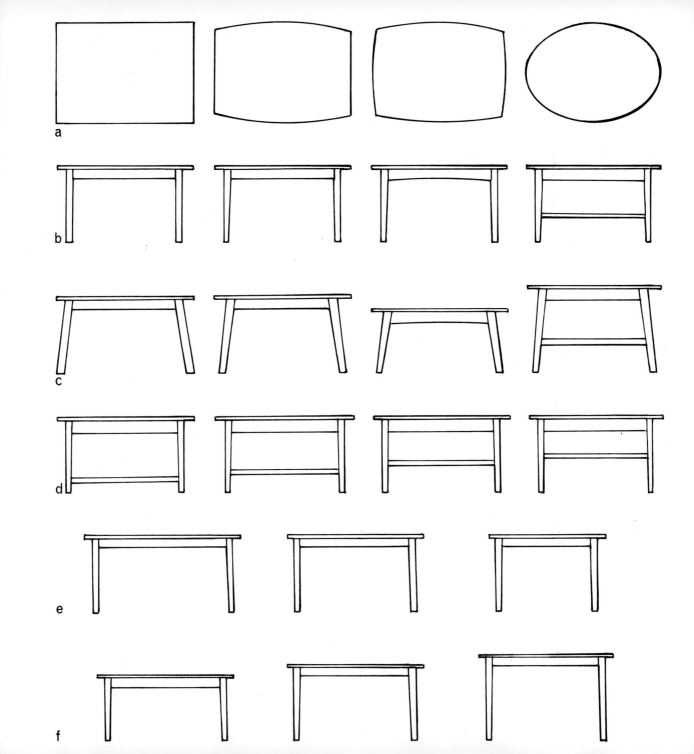

Working drawing

To return to the example of the magazine rack, one of the preliminary sketches will be chosen and drawn out to scale and various modifications made. It is now time to prepare a detailed working drawing. This should contain all the information necessary to make it. See figure *16*.

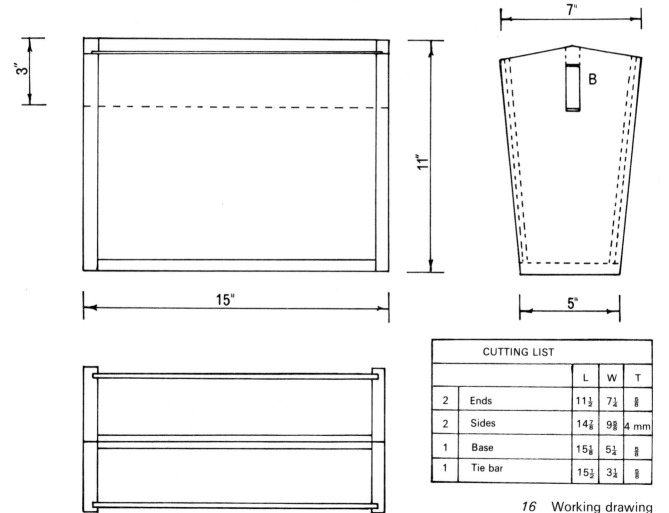

CUTTING LIST					
			L	W	T
2	Ends		$11\frac{1}{2}$	$7\frac{1}{4}$	$\frac{5}{8}$
2	Sides		$14\frac{7}{8}$	$9\frac{5}{8}$	4 mm
1	Base		$15\frac{1}{8}$	$5\frac{1}{4}$	$\frac{5}{8}$
1	Tie bar		$15\frac{1}{2}$	$3\frac{1}{4}$	$\frac{5}{8}$

16 Working drawing

A scale drawing showing three views will give the sizes and show the general arrangement. Using $\frac{1}{8}$ scale (that is $\frac{1}{8}$ in. to 1 in.) will give a very good idea of what the finished article will look like. Around this should be drawn the joint details. It is at this stage that any mistakes can be corrected. If they are left any later they may be expensive in time as well as in material. It will be noticed there have been some alterations to the sizes as a result of all the scale drawings that were made.

To this working drawing should be added a cutting list. All the pieces of wood required are listed with the use to which they are to be put. Having the use noted will allow the selection of particularly attractive wood for such items as drawer fronts and tops. It is usual to make an allowance on the finished sizes for planing the edges and squaring the ends. This is the list which can be handed to the timber supplier.

If the drawing is more complicated and involves difficult curves it will be necessary to make a full size drawing. A dining room chair is a good illustration of this point. The legs are usually curved and a scaled down drawing would not be accurate enough to work from.

Rectangular shapes

Figure 17 shows a number of outline shapes of pieces of furniture. All are rectangular, in some the base is long compared with the height and in others the reverse is true.

In many cases the outside shape is decided by circumstances. The article must contain a certain number of items of a particular size and it has to match the height of another piece of furniture or it has to fit into a recess. This basic shape may not itself be well proportioned or pleasant to look at. The problem is to know how it can be improved.

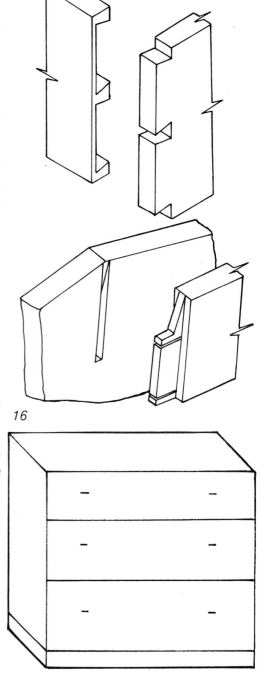

16

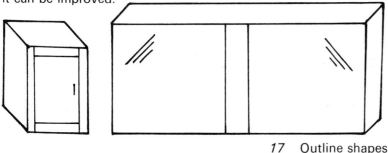

17 Outline shapes

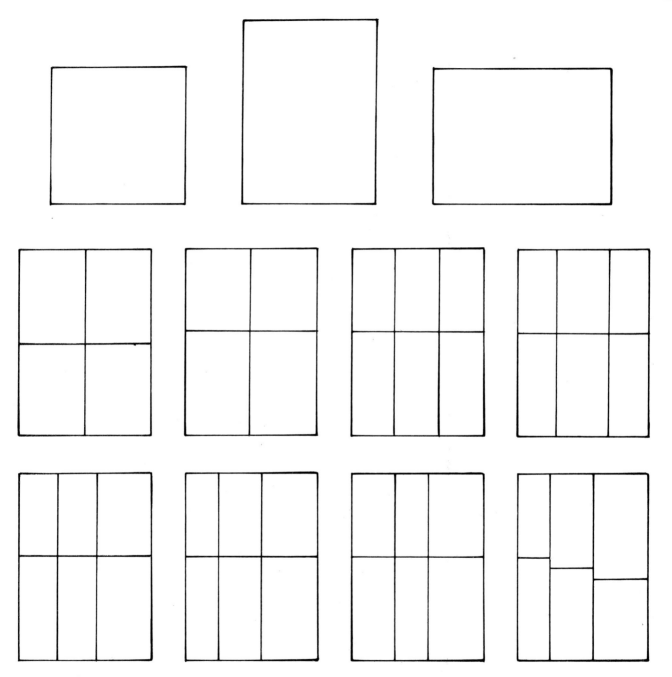

18 The square and two well proportioned rectangles

Figure *18* starts by illustrating a square and then two well-proportioned rectangles, one standing on its long side and the other on the short. Both the latter look very much happier than the square.

The second and third lines take a rectangle and divide it up to see what effect this has. These eight variations are only a few of the possibilities but they are enough to show that the designer has tremendous scope. He can, by altering the internal arrangement, create his own interest.

Figure *19* applies this to a specific problem. A sideboard is required, the length is dictated by the room and the height has also been stipulated. Once again only eight arrangements are shown but many more are possible. It is not essential to have a symmetrical design like (*b*) or (*d*); there is a whole range of other permutations.

Figure *20* turns the line drawings into sketches of sideboards to give a better idea of what they would look like. In this way the designer takes an unpromising shape and improves it by the way he arranges the various cupboards and drawers. There is nearly always something that can be done in even the most difficult and unfavourable situation and it is under difficult conditions like this that the designer shows his true worth.

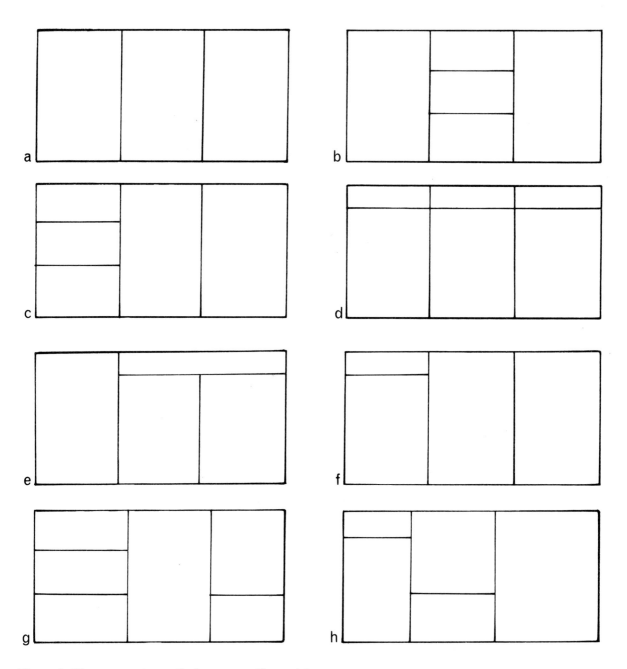

19 a–h The rectangle applied to a specific problem

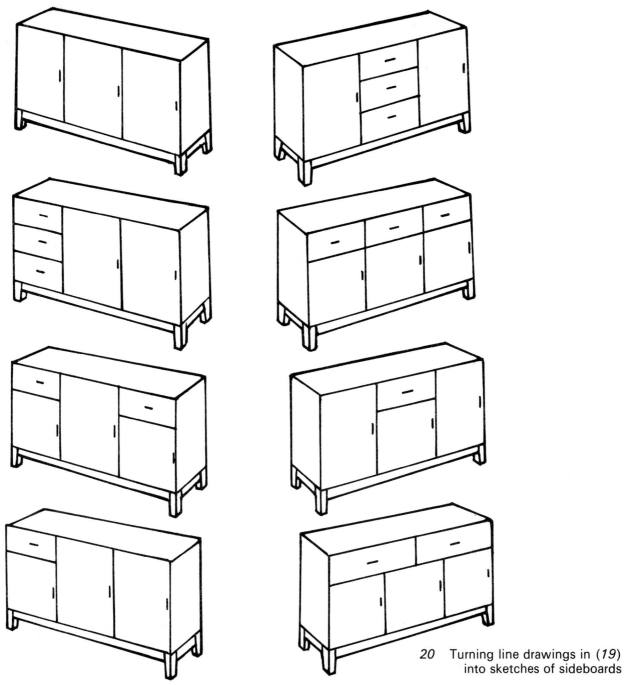

20 Turning line drawings in (*19*)
into sketches of sideboards

Improving unfortunate shapes

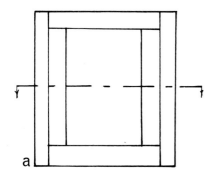

It may well be that even after everything possible has been done the door openings are still badly proportioned, too square, too wide or too high. If a panelled door is used the shaping of the panels can be made to improve the situation. In figure *21a* the opening is square shaped and the panels are only fielded down the sides; (*b*) is a very wide door which could either have two doors or the panel could be divided into two with a muntin; (*d*) illustrates a well-proportioned door with its panels fielded on all sides.

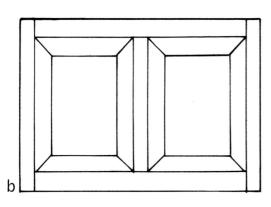

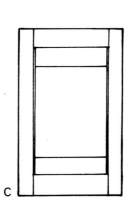

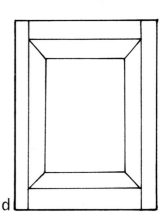

21 *a* Square door panel fielded on sides only
  b Wide door divided by muntin into two panels
  c Narrow door fielded top and bottom only with gap at sides
    to allow for movement
  d Well proportioned door and panel

Designing a book rack

A bookrack makes a very suitable subject for an early exercise in design. It is reasonably small and its function is straightforward and easily understood. Only a limited quantity of wood is required enabling a mock-up to be easily and cheaply made and the completed article itself will not be very expensive. Finally, the hours involved are short and the results, pleasing or otherwise, are soon obtained. At the same time there are plenty of problems to be solved if the finished bookrack is to be worthwhile.

In this section an attempt will be made to follow the design through the usual stages to the point where it tends to get stuck, and take it further until the problem is approached in the abstract. At first the mind is clogged up with the very mediocre bookracks which usually serve the purpose and gradually, if enough time is spent, these can be forgotten and a new approach made.

The first pictorial view shows the usual bookrack in the 'square'. To be quite fair it is extremely functional and will hold books very adequately. The embryo designer is now faced with the problem of how to shape the ends since it is apparent that it would be unsatisfactory to leave it like that. If he is wise he will draw a number of rectangles to scale representing the end and see what he can make of it. If he fancies a curve, he will think in terms of a simple compass curve and figure *22* (*a*) or (*b*) is the result or, if straight lines, then (*c*). With any luck he will not like his efforts and will realise that a compass curve is rarely pleasing because it is monotonous and continuing will come up with (*d*) or (*e*) where an attempt is made to link up the back, top and front edges and make a more unified design. Cutting out a portion of the end could make for an interesting effect as shown in (*g*) and (*h*).

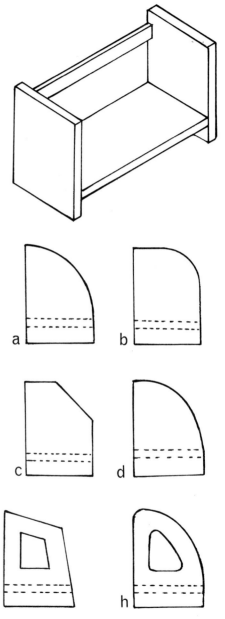

22   *a-w* Designing a book rack

33

The joints can themselves be used as decoration if they are taken through and wedged. (*i*), (*j*) and (*k*) show three possibilities with the wedges inserted in different directions. The tenons could also be made to stand out proud for $\frac{1}{4}$ in. and be chamfered around the edges.

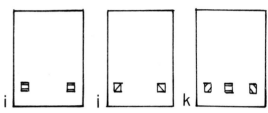

The second pictorial sketch shows another variation. Here the shelf or base is joined with lap dovetails to the ends. This method allows the introduction of feet which can be set in from the ends, as in the diagram, or made flush. These feet can be either parallel strips or they can be tapered from back to front. In the latter case it will incline the whole bookrack slightly backwards.

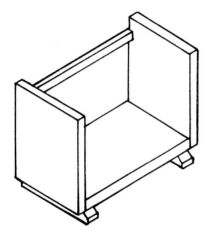

Looking at the front elevation of the bookrack there are several arrangements for the back rail. It could be single and narrow, single and wide, double or even panelled. At this point it becomes clear that the rail could just consist of one narrow rail placed low down. If this is done then the shaping could continue much further round and the 'squareness' of the back edge relieved. Explore these possibilities in figure *22l–q*.

So far the books have been held upright or nearly so, but is this the only way? Would it not display the books to better advantage if they were leaning further back? This arrangement will be less formal and the titles will be more easily read. At first this new positioning is considered within the already accepted construction and (*r*) shows this new arrangement within a blank end, (*s*) and (*t*) show the new freedom this allows.

But why must the conventional construction be used? Draw the outline of the book in its new attitude and decide what is needed to hold the book in that position. There must be a support for the back and front of the book and something to stop them sliding off the end. A possibility is shown in (*u*). This looks as if it might be easily tipped forward and in (*v*) it is allowed to lean back further. (*w*) is a further extension along these lines with only rails supporting the books and here the old image of a book rack has completely vanished.

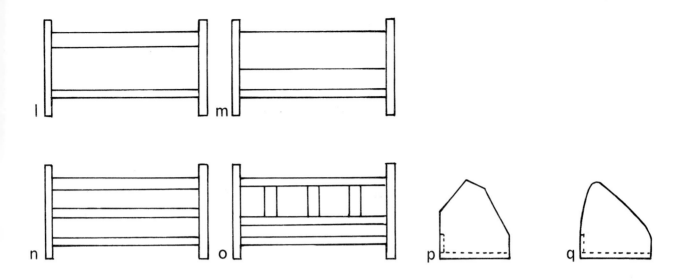

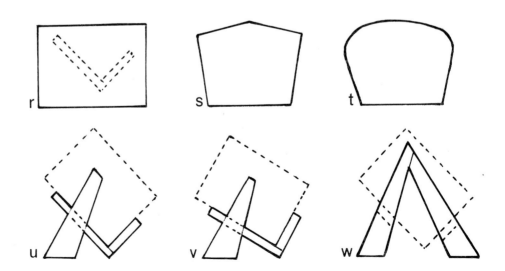

23 A book rack in West African Utile

24 A book rack in Walnut with Sycamore end pieces

25 Easy chair with English oak frame, laminated removable back and re-movable side panels

Designing an easy chair

This project is taken right through from the time when it was decided that this was the next job to be undertaken until the completed chair. This chapter tries to show how the design came into being and the various factors which influenced it and the problems which had to be overcome.

The brief was concise and controlled the design from the start. It consisted of the following eight points.

1   It must be comfortable.
2   It must be easily upholstered and when the time came re-upholstered.
3   To have wooden arms bare of upholstery because these seem to wear quicker than anywhere.
4   The back to have 'wings' to keep off the draughts.
5   The back to be high to support the head in comfort.
6   To be light enough to be easily moved.
7   To be less bulky than the average easy chair.
8   To be stable.

This was a formidable list to include in one design.

A long time was spent on preliminary sketches to try and get an idea of what a chair which answered all these criteria would look like. At the same time it was realised that there are certain essential dimensions which decide whether a chair will be comfortable or not. These will remain the same whatever design is eventually decided upon.

The chair must be wide enough across the front to admit any reasonably sized person. There are then three essential measurements; from the ground to the seat, from the front of the seat to the back, and from the back of the seat to the top of the back. A study of various chairs showed that the second two were complementary. (See *26a.*) Make the depth of the seat greater then the height of the back could be reduced and vice versa. There appeared to be quite a tolerance here. The height from the floor could not exceed a certain figure or the victim would find his legs dangling in space or on the other hand if it was too low his legs would be uncomfortable and tend to stick out a long way. (See *26b.*) These sizes settled themselves easily.

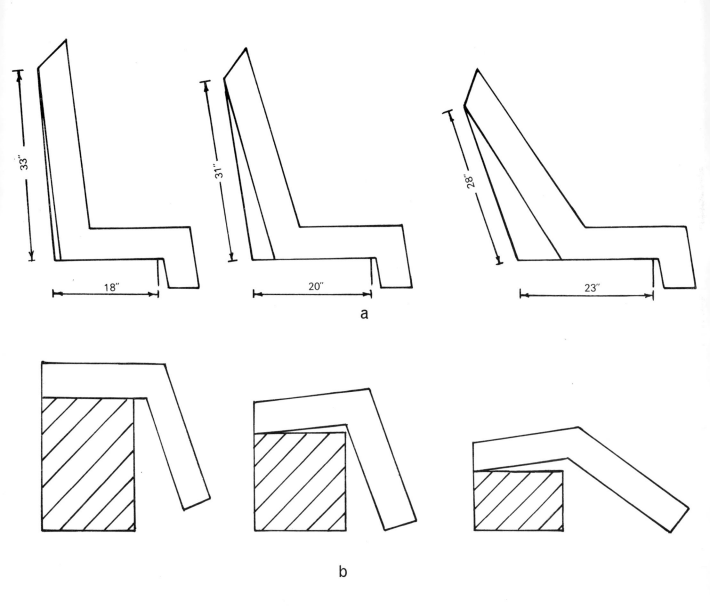

33"   18"

31"   20"

28"   23"

a

b

26   a–b

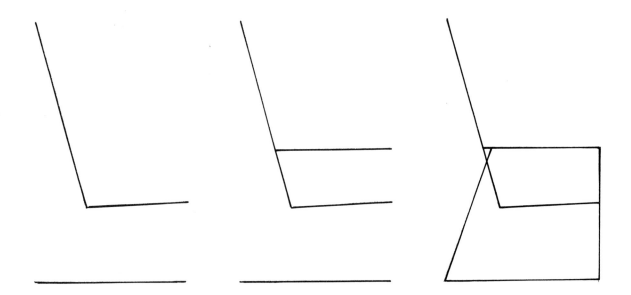

26   c

A lot of scale drawings were now made to get these sizes on to paper and see what they looked like. In the first sketch (*26c*) just the seat and the back were shown in single line. Once the seat height was established this fixed the height of the arms. Legs were added to make a stable chair which would not rock or be liable to tip backwards when anyone sat in it. The back and the arms had now to be considered as a shape to do a particular job; at this stage the constructional problems were ignored.

It was considered essential now to put together a 'mock-up' to test the design as far as it had gone. A chair which looked very fine on the drawing board could turn out to be most uncomfortable when it was made up. A frame was nailed together using any available wood and the various measurements altered until the most comfortable solution was found which fitted into the general plan. There was little to quarrel with at this stage.

There were still many technical problems to be solved before the chair could be constructed. The original idea was to mould a back in fibreglass and this was in fact done. A mould was made of plywood on shaped battens (*27, 28*) and the fibreglass back formed inside. To make the back a sheet of polythene was draped over the mould and a layer of resin applied. On this was

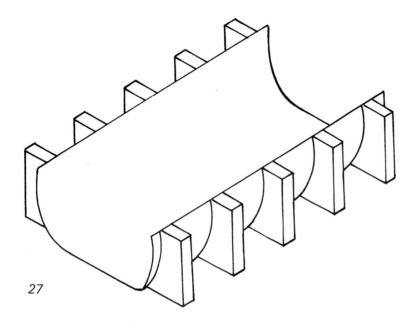

27

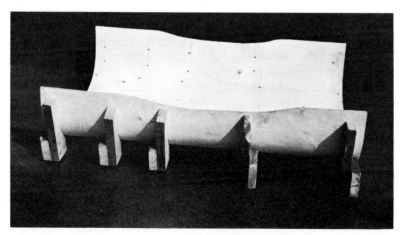

28 The mould used to make the back of the chair

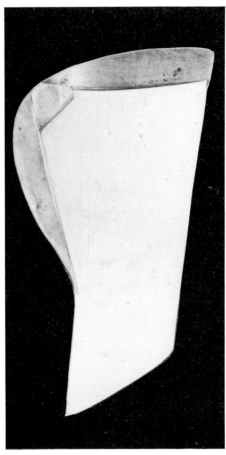

29

laid a sheet of glass mat and a further layer of resin added. Two more thicknesses of glass mat and resin produced the desired thickness. When this was dry it was removed from the mould, the polythene ensuring that it came away easily without sticking. The result was a very strong though springy back with the disadvantage of looking inadequate. This proved to be fairly expensive but it did produce a back of the desired shape. This was very useful used in conjunction with the mock-up and enabled the final shape to be decided upon and the best angle for the back was then found by trial and error.

The sketching was continued in an attempt to fix on a construction which would unite the back and the legs. Finally the idea came of making the arms and the back rail as a unit and then tenoning this into the frame (30a). The only way thought to make the back rail strong enough was to laminate and join the arms with dovetails. This would have the advantage of keeping the joint between the back rail and the arms clear of the top of the back legs. The sketches were now taken to the drawing board and a working drawing made of the frame. This incorporated all the information gained from the 'mock-up'.

It became obvious, at this stage, that the dominant feature in the design would be the shape of the arms and sketch after sketch was rejected until the final shape was arrived at. The widening out inside seemed to suggest both comfort and a welcome while the more sever shaping on the outside matched the rather austere frame (30b).

The frame was now made, although not all the details were yet solved. Enough was decided to enable a start to be made. Once this was done the fibreglass back was propped into position and different angles were tried out until the most comfortable one was discovered. People were asked to sit in the chair and their reactions were studied. They were deliberately chosen so that some were short and others tall in an attempt to discover proportions which would satisfy most people. Once the position of the back was finally established the length of the arms could be ascertained and the arm and back rail unit made up. The back rail was laminated from $\frac{1}{8}$ in. strips around a former and then dovetailed into the arms.

It was realised at this stage that it would not be very easy to upholster the back because of the impossibility of driving tacks

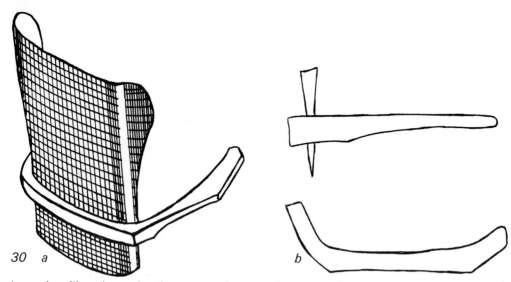

30 a   b

into the fibreglass. At the same time a glance at the mould showed that plywood would take up the shape since it had already been used in its construction. Two sheets of plywood were roughly shaped, glued and cramped into the mould and allowed to set. When they were released they retained their shape and the first plywood back had been produced. It was only 8 mm thick and inclined to be a little 'whippy' as well as looking rather thin and light, although perfectly strong enough for the job. To stiffen the edges and give some thickening, strips of 4 mm Gaboon were glued around the top edge and down the sides to bring them up to about 1 in. in thickness. This was then shaped and tapered from the top edge to the point where the back would meet the back rail (29).

The chair sides were made in a similar way. Curved panels were made by gluing two sheets of plywood together. These were to be held in place by fitting into a groove in the front leg and a rebate on the back (31). They were to be fastened with a screwed batten thus allowing for their easy removal.

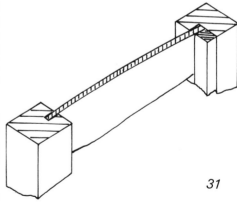

31

The arm unit was secured to the legs with stopped tenons wedged securely from the underside. The back was held in place with four screws into the bottom rail and it was rested on the back rail, there being no tendency for it to come forward. The chair was now put into use for a week. It must be appreciated that a chair that is comfortable for a few minutes may well give the occupant back ache after a few hours! This was the last opportunity to make any minor changes.

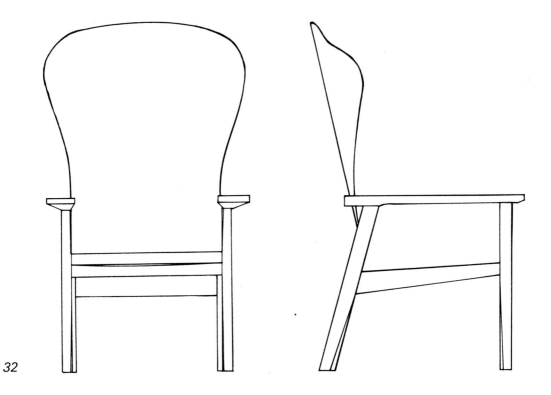

32

The chair, having now passed the test, was ready for upholstering. A 1 in. layer of foam was glued onto the inside of the back. It was not felt that any thicker was necessary because it had been quite comfortable during the test period without anything there at all. The inside was now covered with material which was tacked into the strips which had been glued on to thicken the back. The cover for the back was sewed in place making a seam around the edge. The two side panels were slipped into carefully made 'envelopes' and the two retaining strips secured. With the coil springs clipped into the seat and the foam seat placed on top the chair was complete. Figure 32 shows three views of the completed chair.

3 Joints

Tee joints

33 Half lap. This is a very easy joint to make but is not very strong. Usually reinforced with screws. Used in soft wood frames.

34 Through wedged mortise and tenon. This is an extremely strong joint. It can also be drawn pinned. See 'Bridle joint' *36*

35 Half lap dovetail. The dovetail enables it to be used as a tie

36 Bridle joint. It can be used with or without the draw pin. To fit the pin, holes are drilled slightly out of line so that as the dowel is knocked in it pulls the joint up tight. Commonly used without pin to join centre leg to a plinth

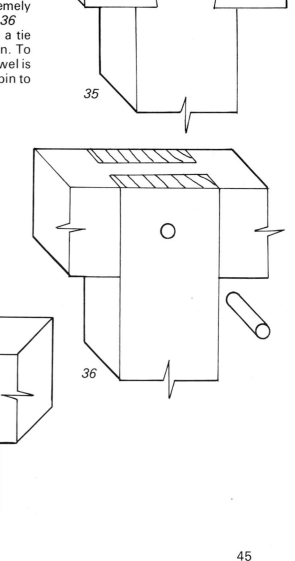

35

33

36

34

Frame joints

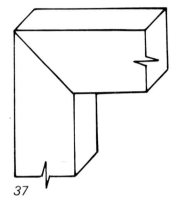

37

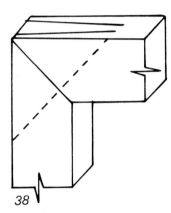

38

37 Simple butt mitre. This is much used by the picture framer and strengthened with a nail across the corner. With the advent of modern glues this is a much stronger joint than it used to be.

38 Veneer key. Here the butt joint is first glued and allowed to dry. Then the corners are sawn at a dovetail angle and the pieces of veneer glued in. If these are a good fit a very strong bond will result

39 Dovetail bridle. This is a joint sometimes used on a heavy picture frame. It would need modifying to take a rebate

40 Half lap. This is suitable for a light frame like a kitchen cabinet door which is going to be strengthened with hardboard

41 Bridle or open mortise and tenon. Not a very attractive joint to use on furniture; it shows too much end grain. Any shrinkage of the rail is also very obvious

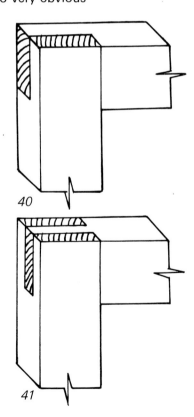

40

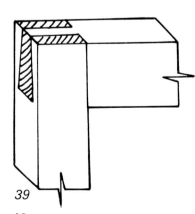

39

41

42 Stopped mortise and tenon. A very useful joint which can have a sloping haunch if it is visible and a square one if it is unsighted. It can be combined with a groove in which case it will require a square haunch to fill the gap left by the groove

43 Long and short shouldered mortise and tenon. If the frame is rebated, to hold glass for example, then this construction is indicated

Carcase joints

44 Pinned and glued. This is only suitable for small jobs where the joint is not expected to take a lot of strain

45 Dovetail pinned. The angle of the nails makes a stronger joint

46 Lapped and pinned. This is stronger than those mentioned above, it is also neater because it hides more of the end grain

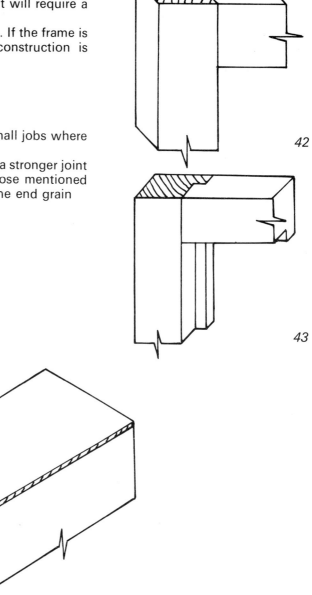

42

43

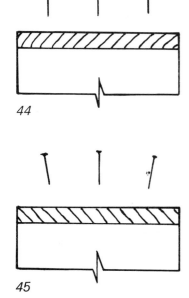

44

45

46

47

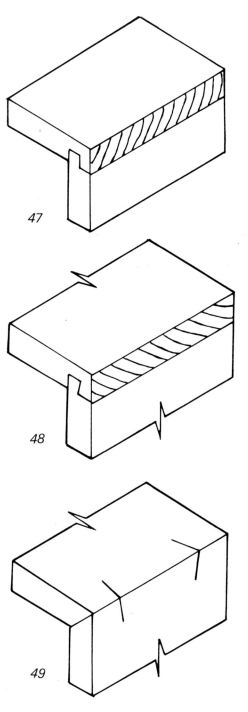

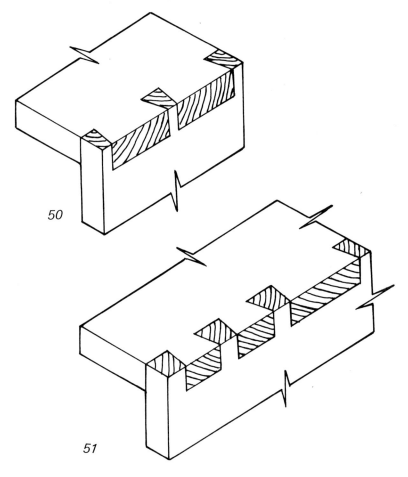

47 Tongue and groove. Used a lot commercially for chess boxes and similar articles

48 Dovetail tongue. This makes a strong practical joint

49 Butt mitre with veneer keys. The keys are added after the butt is glued and set making a very strong and easy construction

50 Through dovetail. A very strong and attractive joint which can be mitred at both or one edge

51 Through dovetail variations. The edge tails are smaller to achieve more holding power where it is most needed. It also provides added interest and this could be repeated on a wide board, i.e. two narrow tails followed by two wide ones. There are other variations which could be adopted

47

48

49

50

51

52 Lap dovetail. This is a suitable joint to use for a carcase bottom where only one part of the joint is visible

53 Lap dovetail. To achieve greater strength at the edges the two outer tails on each side of the joint are smaller to increase the gluing area

54 Secret lap dovetail. This avoids almost all the end grain and the lap can be moulded so that even that little bit is not noticeable

55 Secret mitre dovetail. No joint is visible and it is left to the grain of the wood to provide interest. This is used in high class cabinet work.

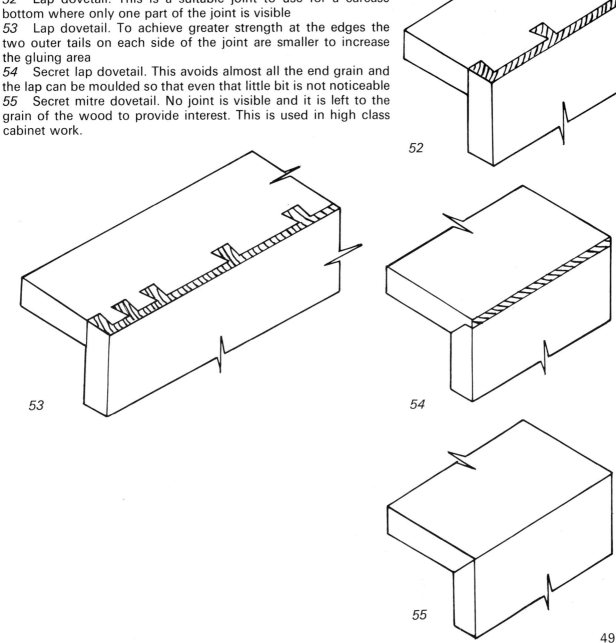

52

53

54

55

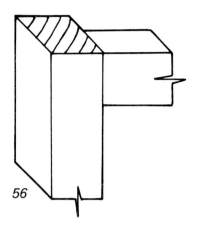

Stool joints

56   *a* Mortise and tenons
      b Tenons mitred to meet rails at right angles
      c Rails over 3 in. wide have double tenons
      d Extra strong thick rails have twin tenons
57   Open mortise and tenon or bridle joint
58   Lap dovetail

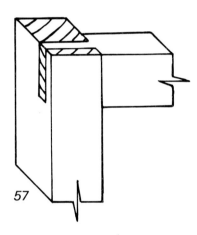

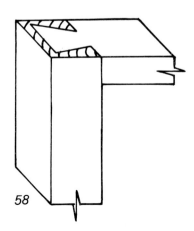

4 Joint construction   Mortise and tenons

Marking out a corner mortise and tenon

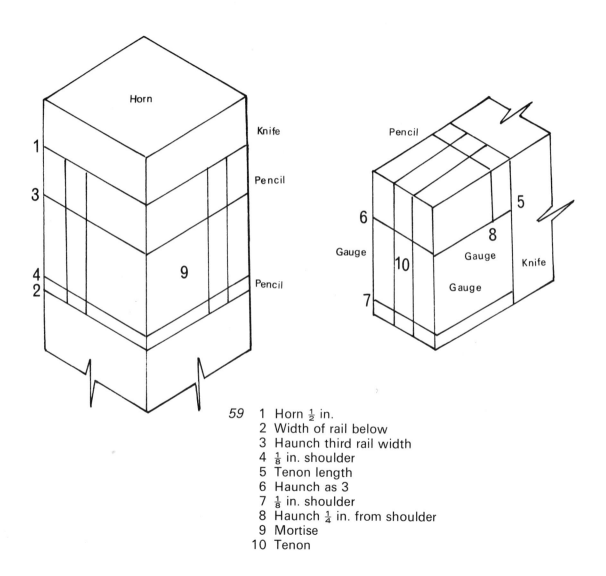

59   1 Horn $\frac{1}{2}$ in.
    2 Width of rail below
    3 Haunch third rail width
    4 $\frac{1}{8}$ in. shoulder
    5 Tenon length
    6 Haunch as 3
    7 $\frac{1}{8}$ in. shoulder
    8 Haunch $\frac{1}{4}$ in. from shoulder
    9 Mortise
   10 Tenon

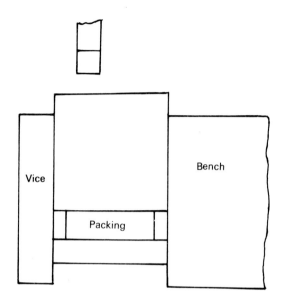

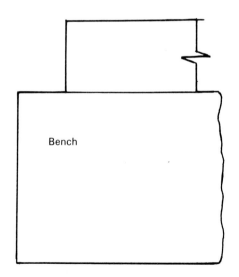

Chopping the mortise

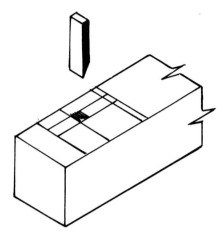

2 Keep each cut as close to the last as possible

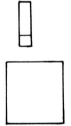

3 Keep chisel vertical and avoid any sideways leaning

4 Mark depth of mortise on chisel with pencil or plaster

60 1 Hold in vice or secure on bench

Sawing the tenon

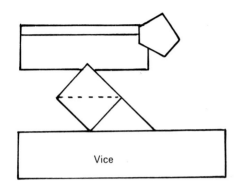

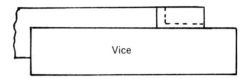

5 Saw across for haunch

61 1 Saw at an angle
2 Reverse and saw again

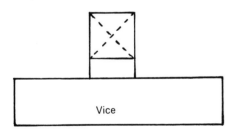

3 Complete the sawing

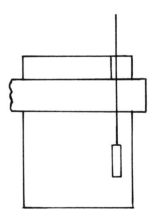

6 Saw shoulders on sawing board

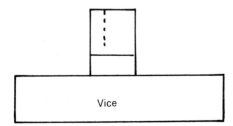

4 Saw down for haunch

7 Reverse and repeat
8 True shoulders with shoulder plane if necessary
9 Chisel haunch to make it slope
10 Fit carefully

Corner mortise and tenon

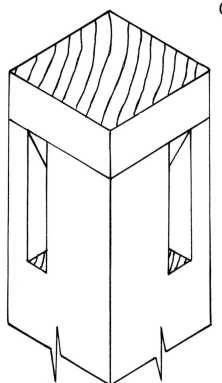

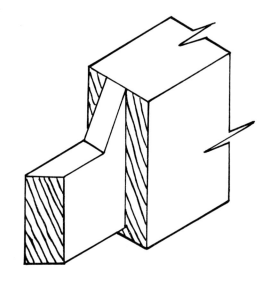

62 Corner mortise and tenon

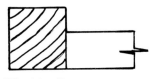

'Flush' rail

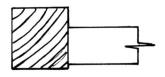

'Set in' rail

Bare faced tenon

Grooved mortise and tenon

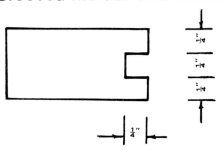

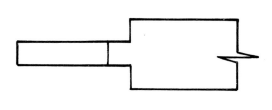

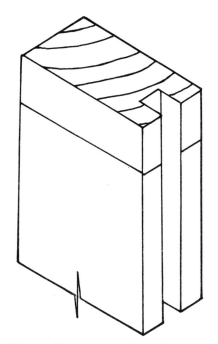

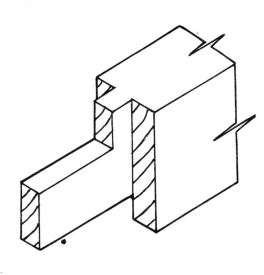

63　1　Mark out as for ordinary mortise and tenon but allow $\frac{1}{4}$ in. shoulder at lower edge for groove
2　Square haunch to fill groove
3　Chop mortise
4　Saw down tenon but do not remove cheeks
5　Work groove on both rails and stiles
6　Remove cheeks of tenon
7　Fit carefully

Long and short shouldered mortise and tenon

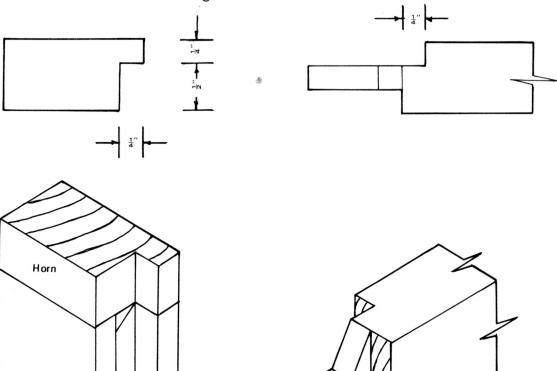

64 1 Mortise hole marked out as for ordinary mortise and tenon
2 Tenon marked out with one long and one short shoulder
3 Chop mortise disregarding rebate
4 Saw down tenons but do not remove cheeks
5 Work rebates on both stiles and rails
6 Remove cheeks from tenons
7 Fit carefully

Faults in tenons

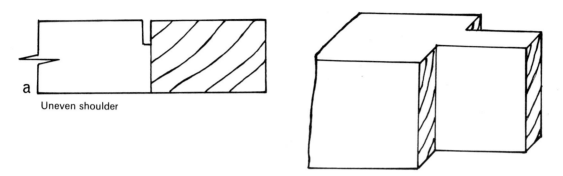

a — Uneven shoulder

65a One shoulder is sawn too much in the waste or on the wrong side of the line

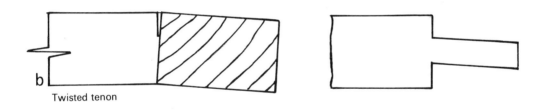

b — Twisted tenon

65b and *c* The tenon is sawn at an angle in one direction or the other or it could be in both directions

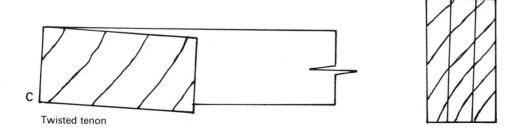

c — Twisted tenon

65d   A too tight tenon forced in is causing end splits

65e   Too thin a tenon

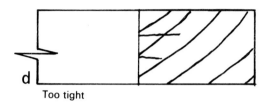

d Too tight

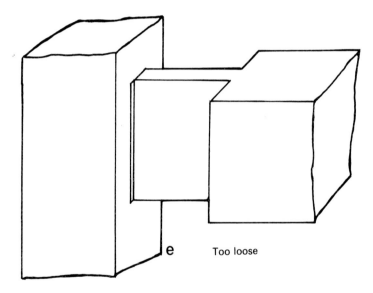

e   Too loose

Method of correction

66a   If one shoulder is too long this is easily corrected with a shoulder plane. If one shoulder has been undercut then the shoulder line must be re-marked when the procedure is as above. If this occurs on a rail with a tenon at each end it will affect all rails of a similar length and they will all need marking to the new length

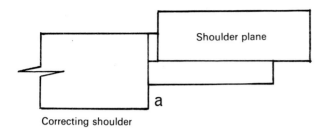

Correcting shoulder

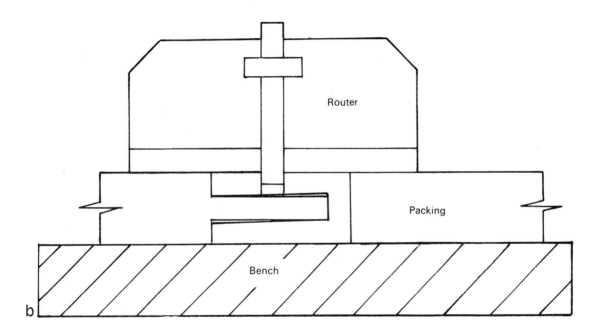

66b   A tenon which is oversize or twisted can be corrected by cramping it on a bench top with a packing piece of the same thickness close by. Use a router across the gap and this will ensure that the tenon sides become parallel to the rail face

This may make the tenon too loose in which case it will be necessary to make up this thickness by gluing pieces of veneer on the tenon sides. Do not attempt to force the saw when sawing tenons since this will make it tend to leave the line and follow the grain.

Faults in mortise holes

The faults illustrated in *65b* and *c* may also be caused by inaccurate chopping of the mortise hole.

While chopping is in progress leave the chisel in the hole every now and then and check with a trysquare that the chisel is going in square (*67*).

Work within the lines and make each successive cut as near to the last one as possible.

Any untrueness must be corrected by paring and this will lead to an oversize mortise hole. Reasonable care in chopping should avoid this problem.

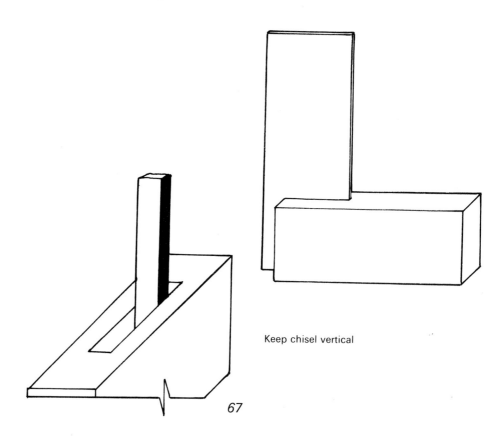

Keep chisel vertical

67

Fitting mortise and tenons

Careful fitting will save some mistakes from taking place.

1 Start by 'offering up' the corners of the tenon to the mortise (*68a*); this will indicate if it is the tenon thickness which is preventing the joint from going home.

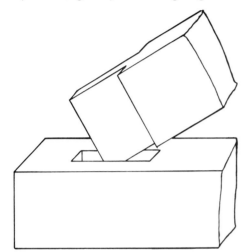

68a

2 The second check is to try the tenon for length. If the tenon passes this test as well as the first then, provided it isn't wedge shaped it should fit (*68b*).

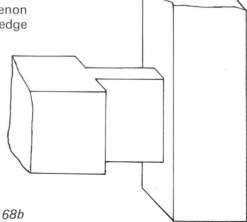

68b

Joint Construction Dovetails

Slope

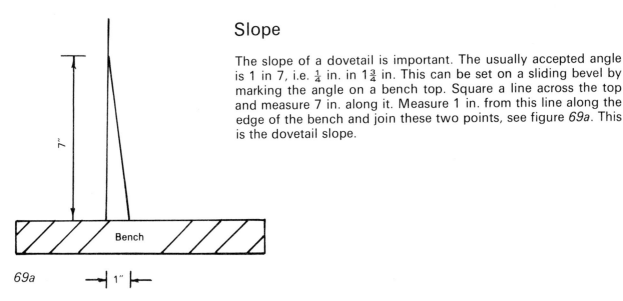

The slope of a dovetail is important. The usually accepted angle is 1 in 7, i.e. $\frac{1}{4}$ in. in $1\frac{3}{4}$ in. This can be set on a sliding bevel by marking the angle on a bench top. Square a line across the top and measure 7 in. along it. Measure 1 in. from this line along the edge of the bench and join these two points, see figure *69a*. This is the dovetail slope.

69a

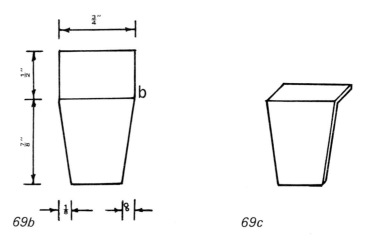

69b

69c

69 b, c A simple template can be made with a piece of mild steel or brass. Cut and file it to size and then bend the top half-inch to a right angle.

Common dovetail

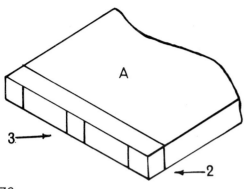

A

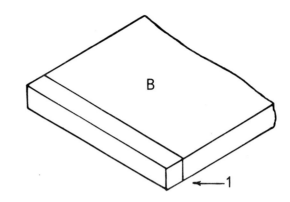

B

3

2

1

70

1 and 2 Cutting gauge set to thickness of wood on A and B
3 Mark out dovetails on end of A with pencil and square
4 Use dovetail template and pencil, also mark waste
5 Place at an angle in vice and saw alternate tails with tenon saw
6 Reverse and saw others
7 Saw corner pins with tenon saw
8 Remove centre pins with coping saw

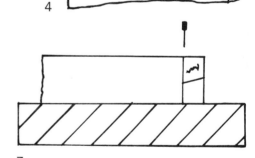

4

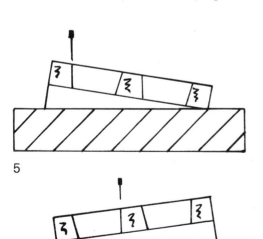

5

6

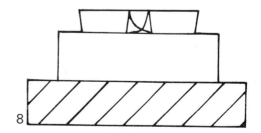

7

8

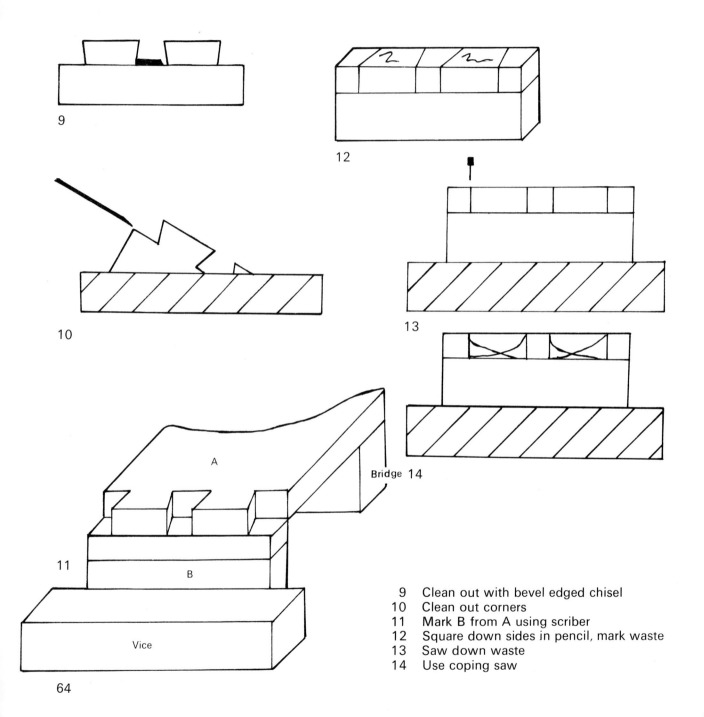

9   Clean out with bevel edged chisel
10   Clean out corners
11   Mark B from A using scriber
12   Square down sides in pencil, mark waste
13   Saw down waste
14   Use coping saw

Lap dovetail

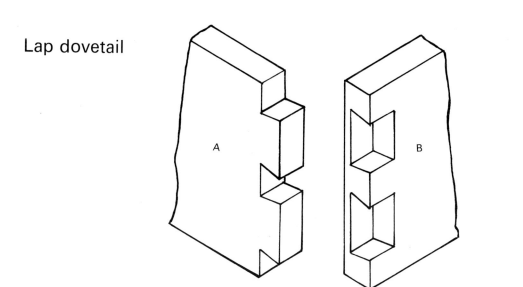

Thickness less lap

Thickness

Thickness less lap

71

1 and 2 Cutting gauge set to thickness less $\frac{3}{16}$ in. for lap
3 Cutting gauge set to thickness
4 Mark out tails and proceed as for Common Dovetail up to 11
12 Square down inside of B with pencil, mark waste
13 Hold in vice and saw down with tenon saw
14 Remove part waste with coping saw
15 Secure on bench, remove waste with chisel and mallet
16 Fit carefully

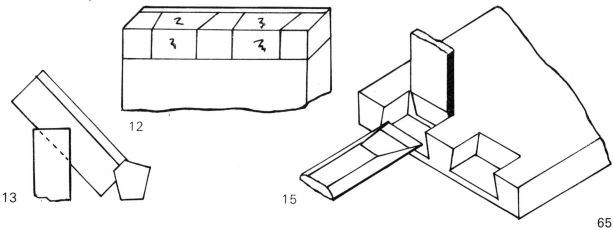

12

13

15

Clean out by paring on to chiselling board on bench (*a*) or on to chiselling board in vice (*b*)

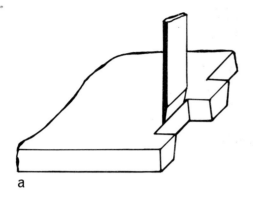

a

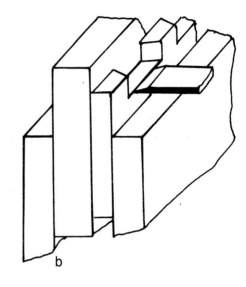

b

Dovetail hints

The recommended way to make through and lap dovetails is to tackle the tails first and to use them as a template. It is essential, therefore, that they should be accurately made.

Checking dovetails

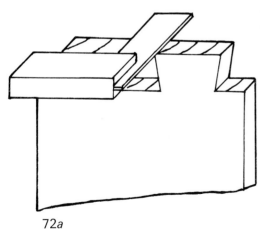

72a   Look at the ends of the tails and check that they are square. A small engineer's square is invaluable for this. If any are inaccurate, place the wood in the vice (*b*) and pare carefully down while maintaining the dovetail slope

72a

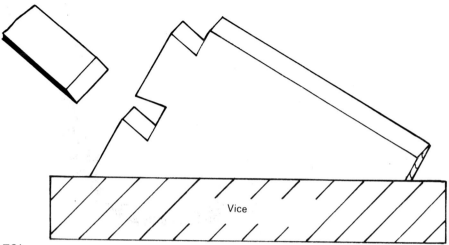

72b

72c The most common fault is to undercut the shoulders as illustrated. A line must be squared round the lowest point and the waste removed. The waste is shown blacked in. This fault should be avoided because the correction will nearly always alter vital measurements

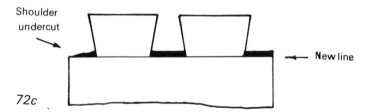

Shoulder undercut

New line

72c

Fitting dovetails

Place the pins in the vice and 'offer up' the tails carefully. Do not remove any wood unless sure that it is the part that is causing trouble. Do not force it into place. A light tap with a tack hammer on each tail will indicate any tails that are sticking by producing a different note from the rather hollow tone of the free joint. Pare down the sides of any pins which require attention and fit again. Repeat until the joint can be pushed together. A too tight joint will cause splitting so do not use too much force.

Secret lap dovetail

Square both ends

1 Set the cutting gauge to $\frac{3}{16}$ in. and gauge lines 1 and 2 on A and B (*73a*).
2 Set the cutting gauge to wood thickness less $\frac{3}{16}$ in. and gauge line 3 on A.
3 Set the cutting gauge to wood thickness and gauge line 4 on B.
4 Mark out the pins on A.
5 Gauge mitres on A and B with marking gauge.
6 Mark out mitre on A and B with mitre square.
7 Mark waste on A.
8 Cut and clean up pins.
9 Work rebate on B leaving $\frac{1}{64}$ in. on the lip to be taken off at the final cleaning up stage.
10 Transfer markings from A to B. Place B flat on bench and cramp A on top with a sash cramp while this is being done (*73b*).
11 Mark the waste and make the tails.
12 Cut mitres and leave a small margin for final fitting.
13 Fit carefully. The lips of B's rebate can be finished off with a shoulder plane.

Note It is essential to make the pins first.

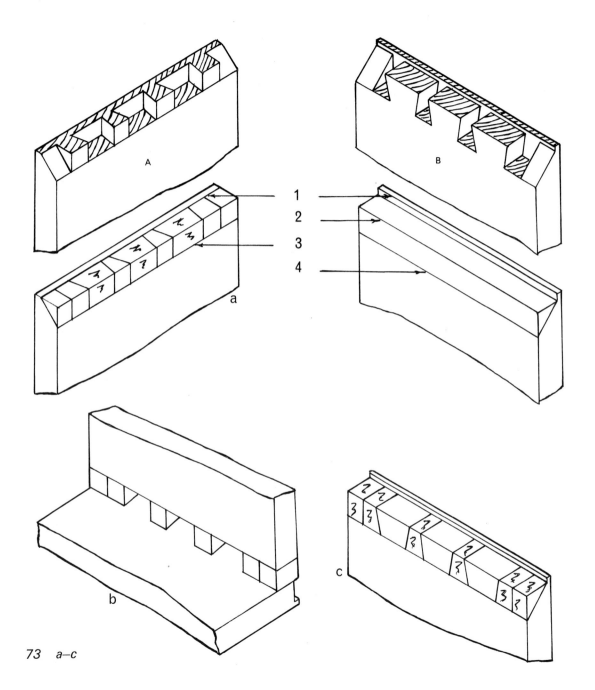

73   a–c

69

Secret mitre dovetail

Square both ends

1 Set cutting gauge to $\frac{3}{16}$ in. and gauge 1 and 2 on A and B (*74a*).
2 Set cutting gauge to wood thickness and gauge 3 on A and B.
3 Work rebates on A and B (*74b*).
4 Mark out tails on A.
5 Gauge mitres on A and B with marking gauge and mitre square (*74b*).
6 Mark in waste on A (*74c*).
7 Make pins.
8 Transfer the markings to B by placing B flat on the bench and cramping A onto it (*74d*).
9 Mark waste on B (*74e*).
10 Make the tails.
11 Work the mitres at corners and on rebates carefully.
12 Fit the joint.

Note It is essential to make the pins first.

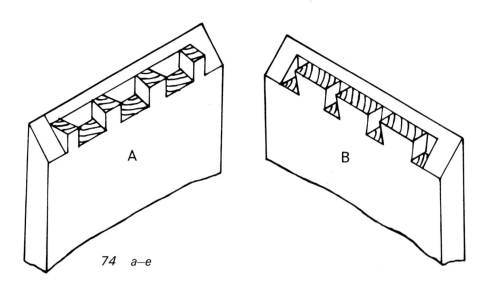

A B

74 a—e

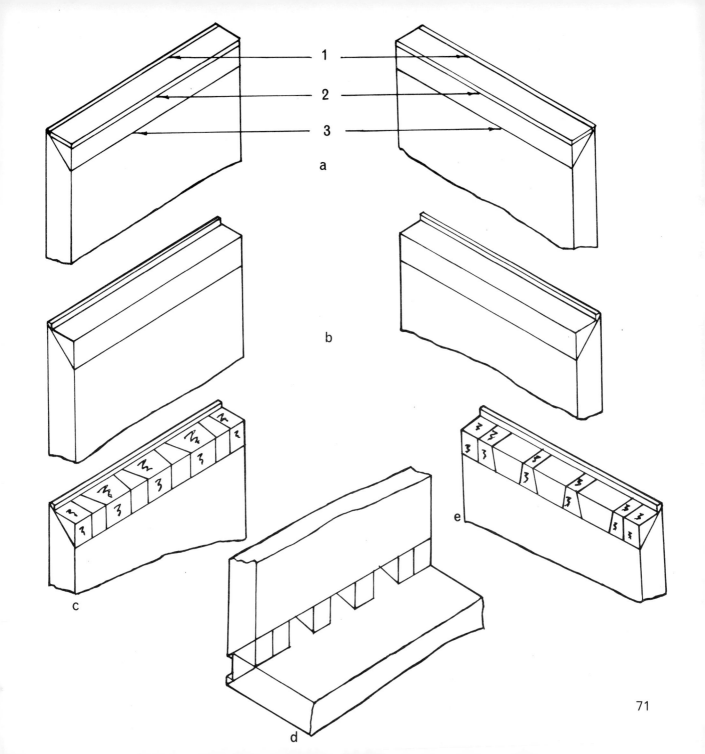

1

2

3

a

b

c

d

e

71

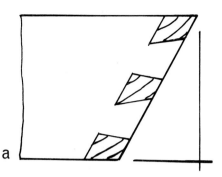

a

5 Special constructions

Angled joints

75 a
1 Through or lap dovetail
2 Either mark out tails from end before sloping at usual slope or afterwards with specially set sliding bevel
3 Make in usual way

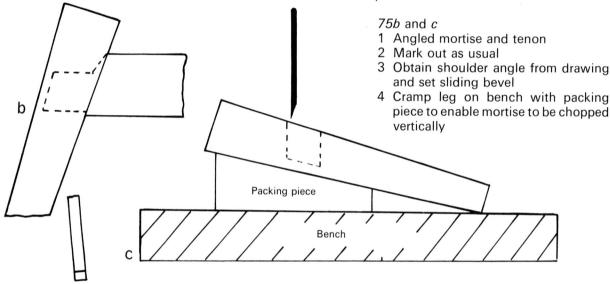

b

c

Packing piece

Bench

75b and *c*
1 Angled mortise and tenon
2 Mark out as usual
3 Obtain shoulder angle from drawing and set sliding bevel
4 Cramp leg on bench with packing piece to enable mortise to be chopped vertically

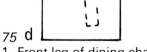

75 d
1 Front leg of dining chair with angled mortise and tenon
2 Cramp on bench and use chisel at angle
3 Set sliding bevel to an angle and use to check as work proceeds

Backs

76a Here the plywood or hardboard back is held in a rebate using either screws or panel pins.

76b Plywood or hardboard can also be held in a groove but in this case it cannot be removed once the carcase is assembled. It also makes gluing up a little more involved.

76c In this example a panelled frame is made up, a tongue worked along the top and two outside edges and the whole thing slid in place and secured with screws. The panel can be simple or fielded. It will be necessary on a wide back to have one or more muntins to reduce the widths of individual panels.

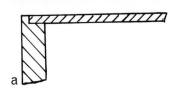

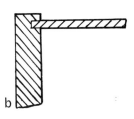

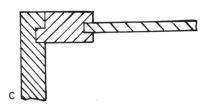

76 a–c
a Rebated
b Grooved
c Framed
  Screwed in place

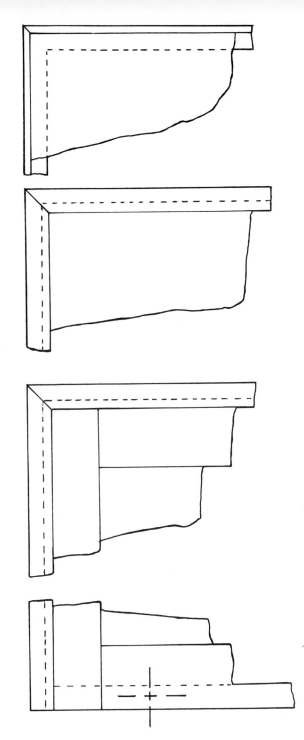

Bureaux

1   *77a* shows the traditional method for hanging a bureau fall. The fall is hinged with strap hinges and a stop prevents it from going in too far.

77b   The panel is made to come nearly flush with the inside, allowing for the thickness of the skiver. An $\frac{1}{8}$ in. of cardboard under the skiver gives a pleasant surface to write on

2   Another method of hanging a fall is illustrated in *77c* and *d*. The fall is pivoted on a metal pin covered with a hardwood plug. This is most suitable for a small hanging bureau, if it was used with a drawer underneath there would be a lot of unusable space because the fall below the pivot moves in an arc as the fall is opened to support it.

3   *77e* illustrates the more traditional method of achieving (*c*) which does not involve more than an inch of waste space.

4   The stationery is usually contained in a separate fitment having the necessary pigeon holes which slides in place after the bureau is glued up.

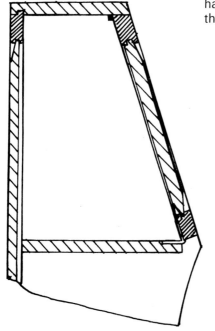

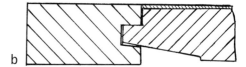

b

77

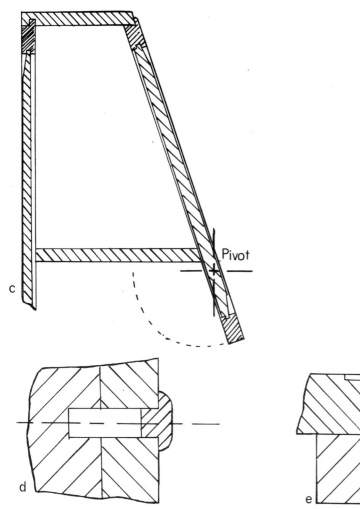

Pivot

c

d

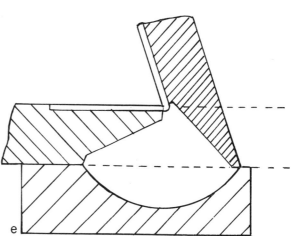

e

Chairs

The method of constructing chairs has changed considerably over recent years. Although these new ideas are very much easier to carry out it is doubtful whether the resulting chairs will last as long as their predecessors. Figure *78* shows three styles of chairs: (*a*) traditional, (*b*) simplified and (*c*) laminated. The following are some notes on the points which have to be considered in each of these types of construction.

78   a

b   c

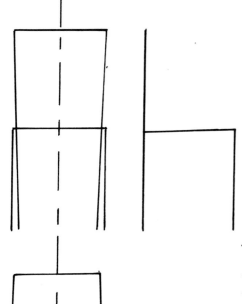

Traditional dining chairs

To give the maximum comfort the seat is slightly wider at the front than the back and slopes backwards while the back is wider at the top and gets narrower as it runs into the back legs. The points are illustrated in figure *79a* in which the plan is shown at seat level. All these factors cause complications which are explained.

a   79

76

Approach

This follows the suggested plan in the design section.

1   Like the chair mentioned in that section a lot of experiment is necessary if the chair is going to be comfortable. Chairs of all sizes should be sat on to see how the body reacts; whether the seat is high enough or, most important, is the back at the right angle and height. Careful measurements should be made and notes taken. It is about these sizes that the chair will be built.

2   Make as many sketches around the basic dimensions, attempting to achieve many different designs, trying to think as freely as possible.

3   Pick out the sketch that looks most promising and draw this to scale. Repeat this scale drawing with a series of minor changes.

4   Amend the scale drawing as necessary and draw it out full size with the front and end elevations and plan superimposed on each other in order to keep the paper a reasonable size. If each view is given a different colour all confusion should be avoided.

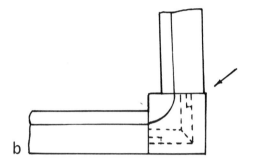

b

Constructional problems

Front legs   These are straightforward with a single rail joining them. Any stretcher rail must be out of reach of the feet of the sitter or it will be continually scuffed. (Stretcher rails are discussed later.) This joint is shown in *79b*.

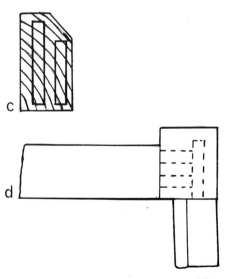

c

Back legs   The main strength comes from a heavy rail at seat height. A chair is subject to a lot of stresses, most of them avoidable if the chair is sat in properly, which must be allowed for. This rail is made thick enough to have two tenons side by side, see *79c* and *d*. To avoid a very heavy look when viewed from the back the top edge is bevelled off.

d

The space at the back can be filled in according to the chosen design.

The legs are thickened in depth at the place where the side rails enter. This shows most clearly in the photograph (*81*).

77

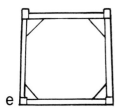

e

Seat The tenons at the front of the side rail are left to run in line with the rails, making the shoulders angled across the width and thickness. The rail is not at right angles to the front leg in either the side elevation or the plan. The mortise holes in the front legs must be chopped at an angle to accommodate the tenons. Notice how the legs are set in a little so that they can be planed off at a later stage to finish flush and in line with the rails (*79b*).

At the back the tenons must run parallel to the axis of the chair otherwise it will be impossible to glue the chair up. At the same time the back legs slope inwards and the tenons must match this slope as well. This back tenon is angled in two directions and the shoulders are also off square. This is shown in *79d* and *30f*. These various angles are all taken off the full scale drawing.

The seat is greatly strengthened by the addition of carefully fitted corner blocks that are fastened with screws a little below the level of the seat rebate (*79e*). The actual seat is composed of a piece of 12 mm plywood upholstered with vinyl material over polyether foam. It is supported by a rebate which runs around the front and both side rails (*79g*). This rebate makes a modification necessary to the tenons which fit the front legs. The square haunch is reduced to a thickness of $\frac{1}{8}$ in. to keep it away from the side of the rebate. It is also stopped $\frac{1}{4}$ in. from the top so as not to show (*79h*).

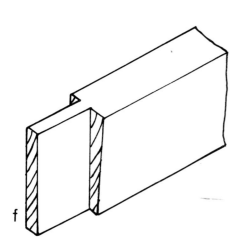

f

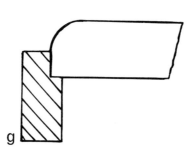

g

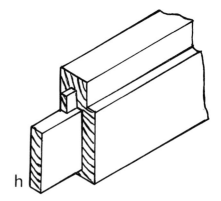

h

Marking out the back rails tenons

If a set of these chairs is required it is worth making two shaped blocks (one right hand and one left) which can be cramped to the rail so that a mortise gauge can be used. The slopes are taken off the full-scale drawing (*79i*).

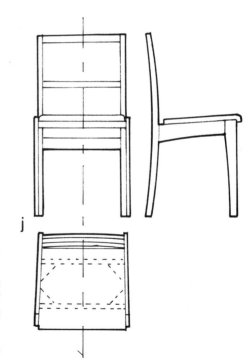

Stretchers These give considerable strength to the chair but care is needed in siting them. To give the most strength they should be as low as possible. In this position they will be scratched and damaged and unsightly. As usual a compromise has to be reached and the rails are kept fairly high with the front one possibly set back out of the way.

Gluing up

The back and front are glued up first and then the completed chair. If the back has a number of splats these may well be glued up separately making two gluings for the back.

Modified dining type chair

Most of the problems which occur in the traditional chair have been eliminated. The seat is still wider at the front than the back but the front and back legs are lined up with the rails. The sides of the chair are glued up first as two frames. The cross rails, which have angled shoulders, are through tenoned and wedged into the side rails. These rails support the seat which is built on a piece of 12 mm plywood and screwed on to them (*79j*). Corner blocks provide extra stiffness.

Here again there are many variations possible using this basic shape and construction.

Laminated chairs

These are extremely easy to make. Once the design has been settled the formers are made (see section seven, which deals with laminations) and the various pieces are formed and cleaned up. The plywood back and seat can be glued on and the legs are screwed to the back rails. One advantage of a laminated construction like this is that it has a springiness built into it which adds to the comfort.

General

Needless to say there are many other solutions which will result in equally successful chairs and those illustrated are merely to show some of the possibilities. Try and tackle the design as just another problem, only in this case it has to support a body and not books or some other articles. Bear in mind that a person, because of his continuous movement and rather careless behaviour, exerts a great deal of stress and that this necessitates a very strong construction.

80   81

80 Dining chair in English Walnut with Sycamore inlay and leather seats

81 This view of the side of the chair shows the extra width of the back leg where the side rail comes in and the arrangement of the under framing with the front stretcher rail well out of the way

Constructions

Ellipse

1   Draw rectangle CDEF with major axis aa' and minor axis bb'. Divide Oa' and a'D into an equal number of parts (say 4) at 1, 2, 3 and 1', 2', 3' respectively. Draw b'3, b'2, b'1 to intersect b3', b2', b1'. These intersections are points on the ellipse. Trace a fair curve through the points and adopt a similar construction for the rest of the ellipse (*82a*).

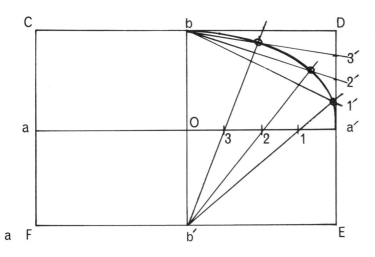

2 *Trammel Method* Draw the major and minor axes, aa′ and bb′. On a strip of paper mark off three points E, G and H, making EG = Ob and EH = Oa. Keeping G on the major axis and H on the minor, move strip into various positions marking the position of E on the drawing. Trace a fair curve through the points.

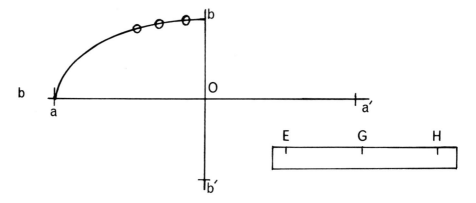

3 Figure *82b* Using cotton or string. Place three pins on f, b and f′, having drawn the axes aa′ and bb′ (bf = bf′ = Oa). Make a loop of cotton and place it over pin f′, keeping the cotton taut, take it round pin b to pin f and wind it round the latter several times, taking care that the loose end is securely held. Withdraw pin b and replace with pencil point. Keeping the cotton taut and the loose end secure, trace the ellipse (*82c*).

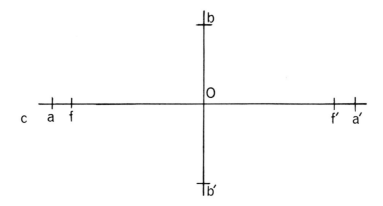

Hexagon

1   Given the length of one side AB, with the compass on A and radius AB describe an arc, repeat this on B intersecting the first arc at O. Using O as centre describe a circle using the same radius. With centre B step off the radius around the circumference. Join these points and the result will be a regular hexagon (*83a*).

2   Given the length of the diameter AB, take a compass with centre A and radius half AB, describe an arc, repeat on B. With centre O and same radius describe a circle. Join the points as shown in figure *83b*.

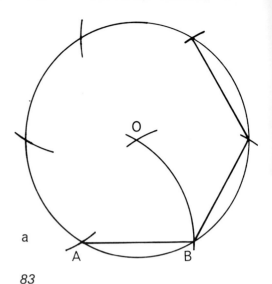

a

83

Octagon

Draw a square of a size to contain the octagon and draw its diagonals. With compass on each vertex and radius half the diagonals describe arcs cutting the perimeter. Join these points of intersection as shown in figure *84*.

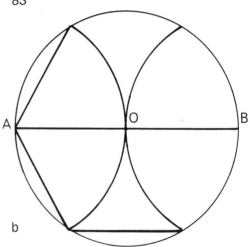

b

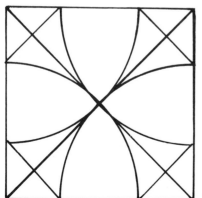

84

Doors

Figure *85a* shows a conventional door composed of stiles, rails, muntin and panels. Like all doors it is best made oversize and fitted to the actual opening when it is completed.

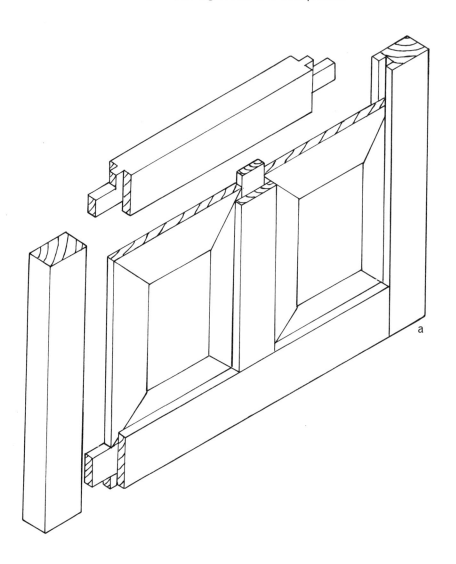

a

85b is a quick construction suitable for a kitchen cabinet. It is made of soft wood with crosshalving joints at the corners which are glued and screwed and then both sides are covered with hardboard

85c can be used where a flush finish is required. Chipboard is used because it is a stable material and within limits any movement can be ignored. It is lipped to hide the unsightly edges which crumble easily and also to provide a firm anchor for the hinges. It will be veneered on both sides

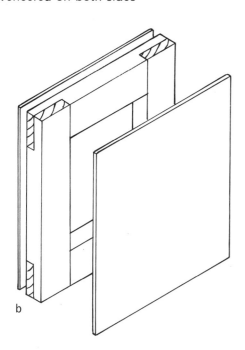

b

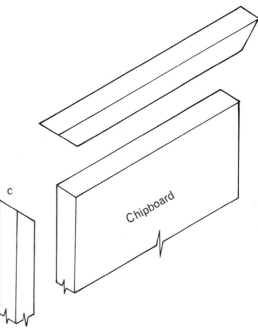

c

Chipboard

Edge joints

It is very often necessary and frequently desirable to join two or more boards edge to edge to make a wide board for a coffee table or some other purpose.

86a is a straightforward 'rubbed joint', that is two accurately planed edges glued together. Modern adhesives make this a very strong joint

86b In this example a tongue and grooved joint has been used. This has the disadvantage that it shows at the ends

86c In this illustration a loose tongue is used. The drawing on the right shows how, if a circular saw is used, the groove can be stopped before the ends and the joint is then hidden

86d It is also possible to strengthen a rubbed joint with dowels but this is not recommended because of the difficulty of lining up the holes with sufficient accuracy

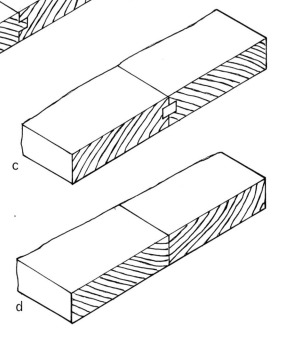

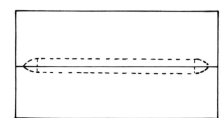

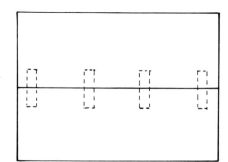

Handles

These are only a few suggested shapes to give an idea of possible scope of wooden handles.

In all the illustrations the tenons have been omitted. These would be turned at the same time as the handles or in the case of the others made as an integral part of the handle and used to hold it while the shaping is being carried out. Because of these tenons the handles must be made with the grain running into the tenon.

At least $\frac{3}{4}$ in. must stick out in order to be grasped.

87a and *b*   These are two drawer handles shown in front and end elevations and plan. They have been left very simple and can both be improved upon

87c is a cupboard handle to match (*b*); again three views are shown

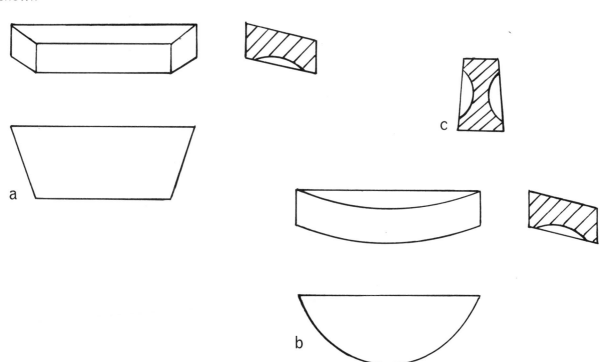

87d The lathe offers a whole range of possibilities. Those illustrated are all finished from the lathe except the second one which has the face chiselled to make a hexagon

87e A wooden drawer handle on a small black bean table

Hingeing

1 Place door in position and mark length of hinge on door and carcase (*88a*), square inside carcase and round edge of door.
2 Set a marking gauge to thickness 't' and gauge door stile.
3 Set a marking gauge to width 'w' and gauge inside carcase and edge of door.
4 Remove the waste from the door with a saw and chisel and from the carcase with a chisel.
5 Screw the hinge on the door.
6 Screw the door in place using only one screw to each hinge. Check the swing of the door and if satisfactory complete the screwing. If not adjust one of the hinges using another screw hole until satisfied.

It is customary to fit hinges to a cabinet so that the top of the top hinge and the bottom of the lower one are in line with their respective edges of the door stiles. If it is a flush door then they will be their own length in *88b*.

There are two usual methods of securing the hinges. *88c* is the best method with the hinge set in at an angle so that each leaf is partly set in either the door frame or the carcase. *88d* shows an alternative method with the hinge entirely cut into the door frame.

Box lids either have the hinge set out as in *88e* or let in flush as *88f*. In the latter case the hinging edges of the lid and bottom must be bevelled to allow the box to open.

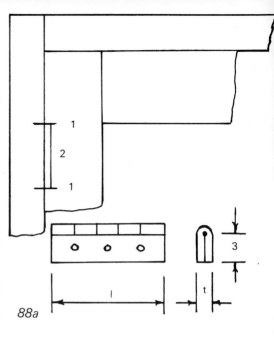

88a

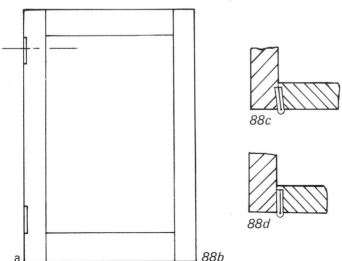

88b

88c

88d

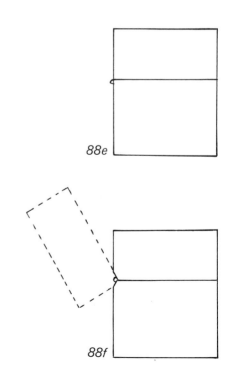

88e

88f

Lids, box

Figure *89a* shows the method of making a box and lid in one. This ensures a perfect fit when they are separated. The pin which coincides with the join between the lid and the bottom is made double size plus an allowance for a saw cut and cleaning up. The box is glued up with the top in place, the bottom is screwed in place and then the box is sawn into two. *89a* shows a tool chest where the top and bottom will be screwed on and *89b* the same construction applied to a jewel or cigarette box with top tongue and grooved and bottom rebated and screwed.

89c   This box has a sliding lid and two corners of the dovetails are mitred to accommodate the groove

89d and *e*   These are two types of drop in lid. *89d* is only suitable for a very small box, while *89e*, having battens to locate it, will be prevented from warping and could be a little bigger

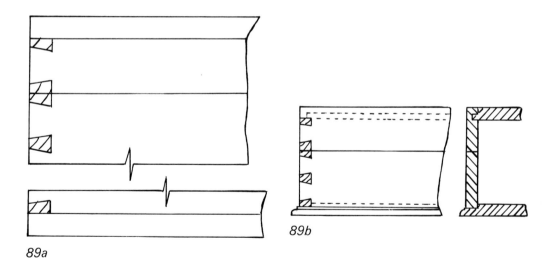

89a

89b

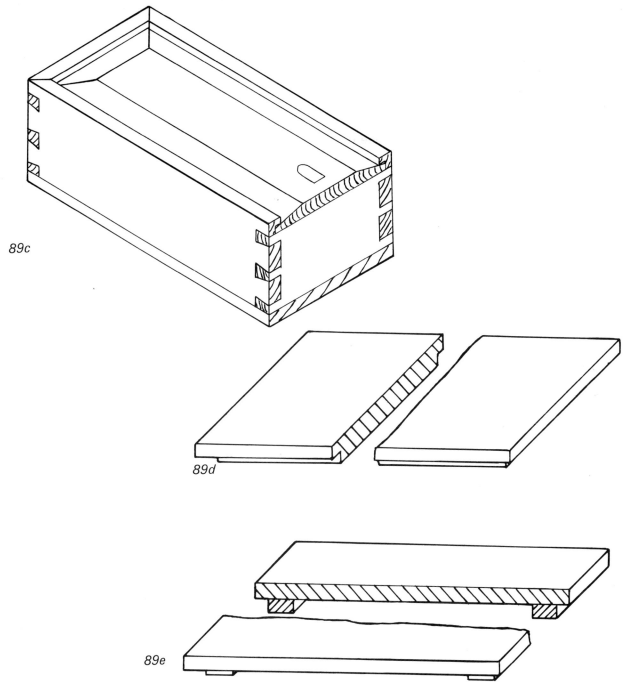

89c

89d

89e

91

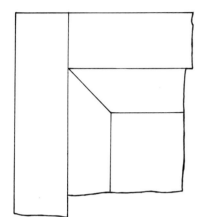

Panels

There are various forms that a panel can take and four of them are illustrated here.

90a shows the most common one with a rebate

90b   If the panel is too thin it can be made without a rebate but this is more difficult since the line has to be achieved by accurate planing. Care must be taken not to round this line when glass papering

90c is a flush panel usually reserved for somewhere out of sight

90d   This is an overlaid panel and requires a thicker board. The moulding is worked with a shoulder plane after it has been defined with a cutting gauge

90a

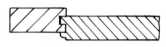

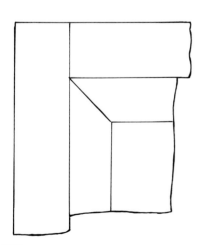

90b

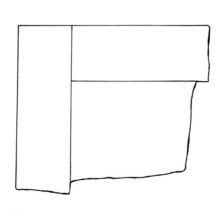

90c

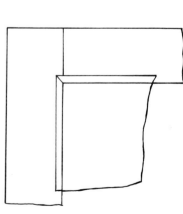

90d

Plinths

As a general rule they should either fit right down to the ground or high enough to clean under. It is almost impossible to clean with less than 4 in. clearance.

The plinth is there to provide some means of protection from kicks accidentally given during normal use.

91a shows an outline sideboard with a framed plinth

1   This is of a simple mortise and tenon construction.
2   The rail is slightly reduced in width at the centre to improve the appearance.
3   The plinth is set in at the back to allow for the skirting board (see side elevation).
4   A large sideboard or other piece of furniture might require a centre leg to provide additional strength.

91b   Here a solid plinth with a dovetailed construction is used. This is usually reserved for small cabinets

91c   In this example the solid sides are continued right down and a false piece inserted to fill the space below the bottom shelf

91d   The plinths are normally buttoned on

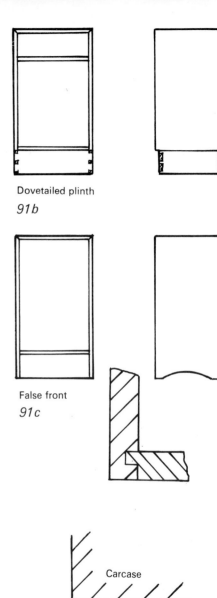

Dovetailed plinth
91b

False front
91c

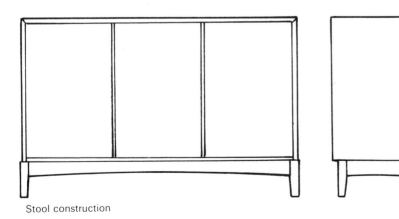

Stool construction
91a

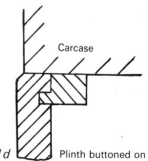

Carcase

91d   Plinth buttoned on

Shelving

Shelves can either be fixed, in which case they add greatly to the strength of the construction or they can be adjustable and give a degree of flexibility to their possible arrangement.

Figure *92a* and *b* show fixed constructions. The mortise and tenon with housing should always be stopped at the front but the housing could be continued right through at the back. The tapered dovetail housing is a very strong joint which has the effect of tying the two sides together.

Figure *92c*, *d* and *e* are methods of allowing for adjustable shelves. The fittings for *92d* are easily obtained.

For a small job like a shaving cabinet it will be sufficient to screw two battens to the sides and let the shelf rest on top.

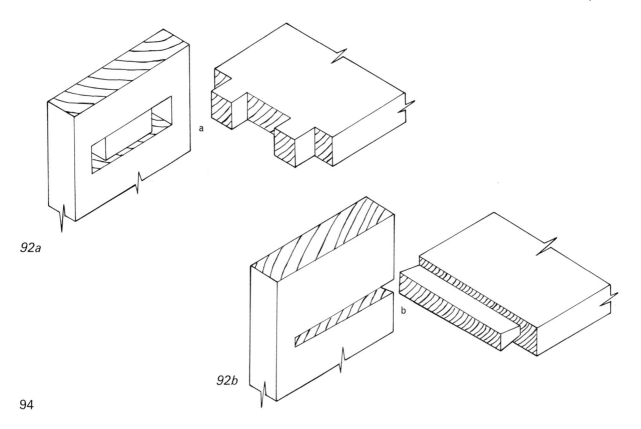

92a

92b

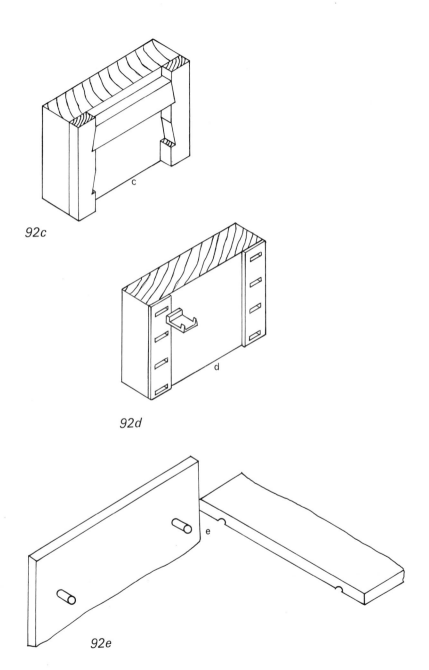

92c

92d

92e

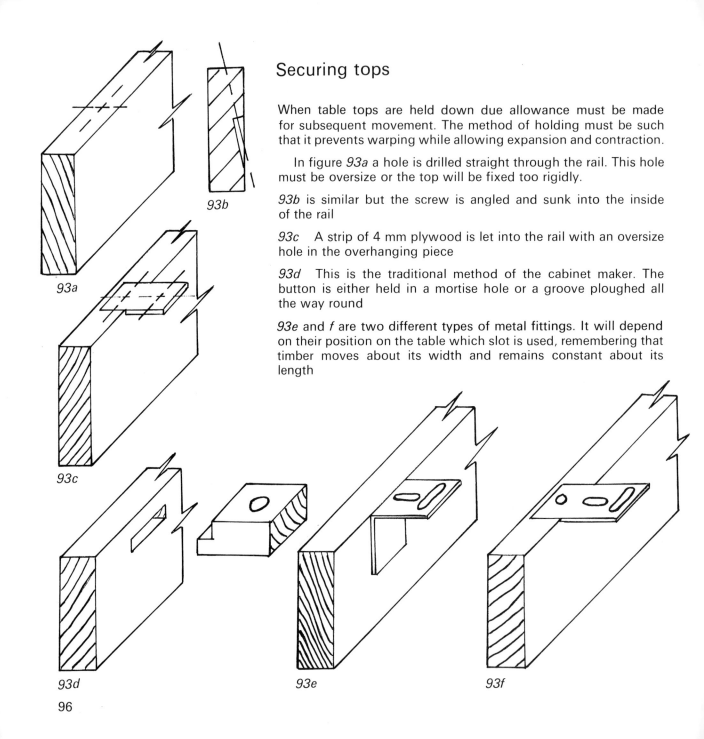

Securing tops

When table tops are held down due allowance must be made for subsequent movement. The method of holding must be such that it prevents warping while allowing expansion and contraction.

In figure *93a* a hole is drilled straight through the rail. This hole must be oversize or the top will be fixed too rigidly.

93b is similar but the screw is angled and sunk into the inside of the rail

93c   A strip of 4 mm plywood is let into the rail with an oversize hole in the overhanging piece

93d   This is the traditional method of the cabinet maker. The button is either held in a mortise hole or a groove ploughed all the way round

93e and *f* are two different types of metal fittings. It will depend on their position on the table which slot is used, remembering that timber moves about its width and remains constant about its length

93a

93b

93c

93d

93e

93f

93g Where a cabinet is made with the 'false top' construction, that is rails lap dovetailed into the sides instead of the top being jointed, the top is secured by screwing through the rails. This should be done at a slight angle to allow a screwdriver to be used, especially if there is a shelf just underneath

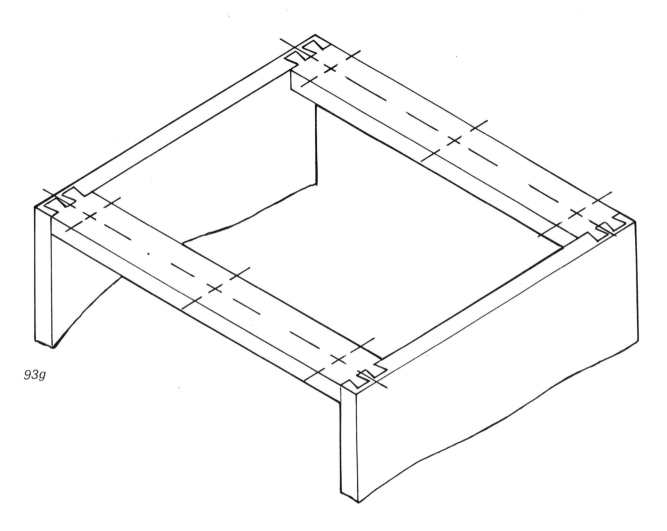

93g

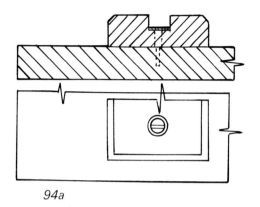

94a

Warping—*Keeping boards flat*

Figure *94a* shows the usual way of keeping a drawing board flat. The boards are arranged with the grain deliberately at random to counteract the tendency to warp. The battens are then slot screwed onto the back. Each of the holes through the batten and the washers are slot screwed so that the round head screw can slide and allow for any expansion and contraction.

94b is the old-fashioned type of pastry board and is also used on the cheaper drawing boards. This is known as clamping

The next shows a framed construction where the panel is made to lie flush with the stiles and rails. There will have to be a gap left at the sides of the panel to allow for movement.

The method shown in *94d* is extremely neat and effective. First of all two strips are sawn off the edges. Then tapered dovetail keys are inserted and the strips glued on again. The keys are made a little shorter than the width of the middle piece of panel.

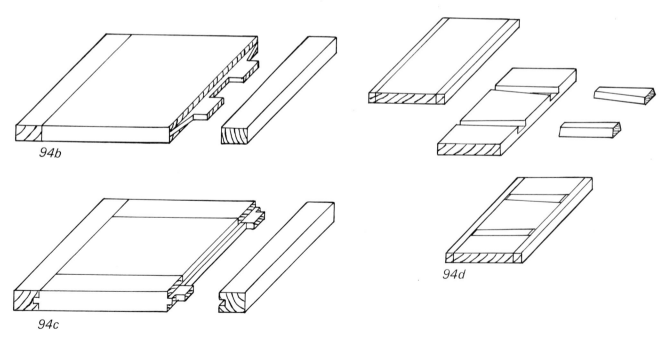

94b

94c

94d

6 Drawers

Drawer construction

Drawers are not difficult to make if tackled in the right way. Such a method is laid out in note form. It will be seen that there are two different shaped drawer slips in the diagram. Which of these to use is decided by the use to which the drawer is to be put. If it is for stationery that requires to be kept flat then the top one is recommended, otherwise the rounded one is used. The rounded slip makes the tongues on the bottom in the same position both back and sides. The tongue is always at the top of the front edge to avoid any possibility of a gap showing inside the front of the drawer.

It is a good idea to leave the thickness of the drawer sides $\frac{1}{32}$ in. full instead of planing right down to the gauge line. This makes cramping up a lot easier because the tails at both back and front will stand proud and allow a cramping block to be laid straight across. When the drawer is glued up and ready for fitting the sides can be planed down. A heavy baulk of timber should be fastened to the bench with the end hanging clear. The drawer side can be supported on this while it is planed.

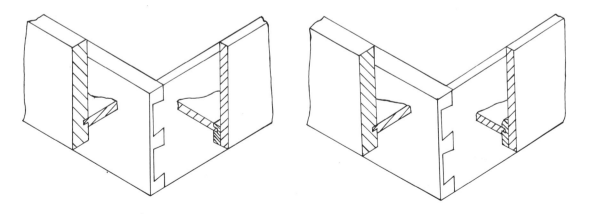

95   Diagram showing the tongue on a drawer bottom and the position of the groove in the drawer front and slips

Drawer construction

1   Leave drawer sides $\frac{1}{32}$ in. full in thickness.
2   Make drawer sides wide enough to include drawer slips.
3   Plough drawer slips while still attached.
4   Gauge and remove drawer slips.
5   Plane drawer sides to fit opening and letter 'Left' and 'Right'.
6   Plane front to fit opening end to end but leave width $\frac{1}{8}$ in. full.
7   Plane back to fit opening end to end and required width ($\frac{3}{16}$ in. less than width of sides).
8   Square ends of drawer sides.
9   Mark out lap dovetails and make and fit to front.
10   Mark out and make through dovetails at back.
11   Round off top edge of back. Take off top back corners of sides.
12   Chop mortise hole for handle in drawer front.
13   Clean up and polish inside omitting to polish where drawer slips are to be glued.
14   Glue up drawer.
15   Make bottom and work tongues (grain to run across drawer).
16   Hold slips onto ends of bottom and present to drawer frame.
17   If too wide, fit by planing off outside of drawer slips.
18   Glue slips onto drawer sides.
19   Fit bottom and, after polishing, glue into groove at front of drawer and leave dry in slips, slot screw into drawer back.
20   Fit drawer to opening.

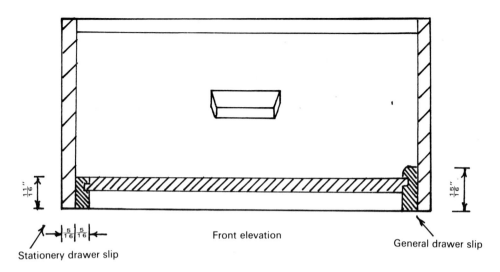

$1\frac{1}{16}''$

$1\frac{5}{16}''$

$\frac{5}{16}$ $\frac{5}{16}$

Front elevation

General drawer slip

Stationery drawer slip

96 a Drawer construction front elevation

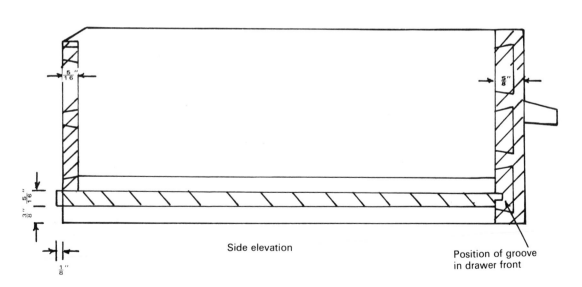

$\frac{5}{16}''$

$\frac{5}{16}''$

$\frac{3}{8}''$ $\frac{5}{16}''$

$\frac{1}{8}''$

Side elevation

Position of groove
in drawer front

96 b Drawer construction side elevation

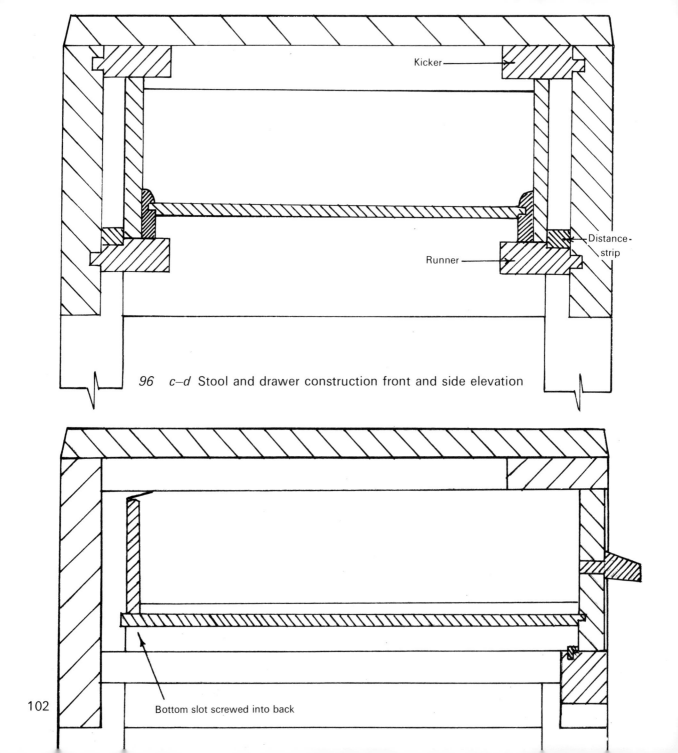

96 *c–d* Stool and drawer construction front and side elevation

Kicker

Distance-strip

Runner

Bottom slot screwed into back

Drawer framing

The construction to support a drawer can be complicated since a drawer requires three things if it is to run smoothly. It must be supported from underneath, there must be something to act as a kicker to prevent the drawer from dropping as it is withdrawn and there must be some means of preventing sideways movement.

If the drawer is going into a solid construction then there is no problem. All the conditions are satisfied without any additions (*97a*).

If, for reasons of economy, a frame is used to take the place of the solid shelf then allowance must be made for the expansion and contraction of the sides. The grain of the frame will be opposed to that of the sides. The front and back rails are tenoned into the sides and the side rails glued into the front. A gap is left at the back and a dry hardboard tongue inserted (*97b*). A similar method is used for the false top construction (*97c*).

It may be needed to fit a drawer into a stool construction and the method is shown in a series of diagrams where the drawer can be seen fitting into its position. This arrangement allows the rails and kickers to be glued in place at a second gluing after the main frame has set. The drawings show clearly the distance pieces that make up the difference in thickness between the legs and the side rails. The drawer stop is made with the grain running in the direction of the tenon.

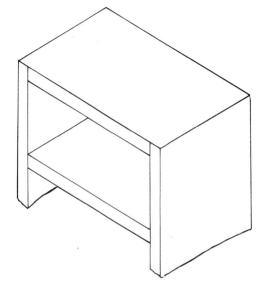

97a   Solid construction

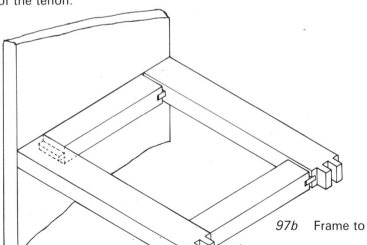

Kicker

Loose tongue and gap

97c   'False top' construction showing loose tongue

97b   Frame to support drawer

103

Flush front drawer construction

Sometimes a design calls for all the drawer fronts to present a flush surface. The drawer fronts can then be matched up for grain or else veneered with matching veneers to give a very smooth appearance. Figure *98* shows three methods of doing this.

98a This can be made by making the drawer with the front $\frac{3}{16}$ in. thinner than usual and with through dovetails at the front instead of laps. The $\frac{3}{16}$ in. can now be glued on to form the rebate all round. It could also be made by using wood the normal thickness and making the rebate first and then making the joints

98b has the drawer sides secured with tapered dovetail housings

98c has a simple housing

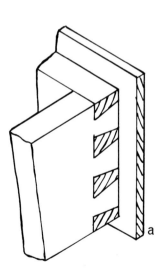

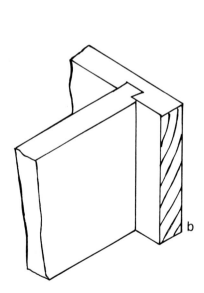

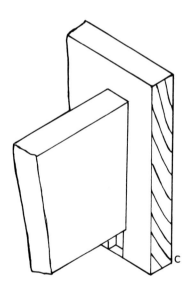

7 Laminating

Wood has natural limitation; it is strong about its length but weak about its width. This is common knowledge and who would make a see-saw with the grain running the wrong way? This weakness is clearly seen in a saw and the craftsman will be aware of the reason for the insertion of a length of dowel rod through the short grain in the handle. The shipwrights who years ago built wooden ships were aware of this and when they had need of a curved member they chose a tree with a natural curve which matched the one they were after.

The modern craftsman can follow the old method and select his wood so that the grain follows the desired curve but this is not easy and would require a large stock of timber being held. It is also inclined to be a very wasteful method, leaving a lot of odd shaped offcuts.

The modern solution is to laminate. If a timber is sawn into thin strips these will usually bend quite easily. The thickness is built up with a number of these strips and if they are cramped in the desired shape when the glue is dry they will retain their shape. The grain in all strips runs along their length and so maximum strength is achieved.

The major part of the work involved in laminating comes in the making of the formers. These must be very accurately made because the resulting lamination will repeat every bump, bulge or inaccuracy. If only a moderate curve is required then a solid block of wood will be adequate (*99a*), but heavier and more curved members will require a more elaborate former (*99b*). It is a good idea to always make the former at least $\frac{1}{4}$ in. wider and 2 in. longer at each end than is absolutely necessary. This will help to ensure that the edges and the ends are adequately glued. If a large surface is to be laminated, as for example the chair backs in Part 2, then a frame has to be made and surfaced. In this particular case plywood was used for this purpose.

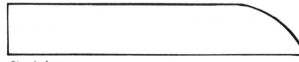

Simple former

99a

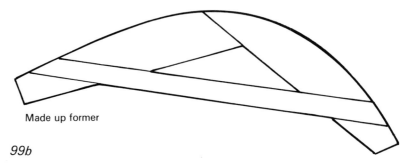

Made up former

99b

When the strips are held against the former for gluing some method must be adopted to transmit the pressure of the cramps evenly along the whole surface. One method is to make both a male and female former (see *99c*). An alternative and easier method is to use a flexible steel blade which will take up any curve used. A length of old band saw blade 3 to 4 in. wide is excellent for this purpose. It is advisable to grind off the points of the teeth before using it to avoid a nasty accident

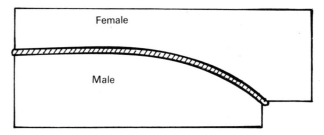

Two part former

99c

Having made the former it is cleaned, glasspapered, coated with two layers of shellac and glasspapered again. A layer of wax polish will help to ensure that the completed lamination will come away easily when the glue is set. As an additional precaution strips of waxed paper, such as that used to line cereal packets, are placed on either side of the laminations between both the former and the steel band

A two part resin glue is recommended for this work. It is extremely strong and allows sufficient time to get the whole thing cramped up before gelling starts. Spread some newspaper on the bench and lay out the laminations. Letter them as shown in

G	1	
G	2	H
G	3	H
G	4	H
	5	H

Strips marked for gluing

99d

99d with a large G to indicate that that is the side to glue. (Notice that the last piece has no letter G.) Now turn over and letter with an H as indicated in the figure, this time omitting the first piece

Tie some rag round a stick and apply the hardener to the strips lettered H. Turn them over when this has been done and apply the glue to the marked strips. To make sure that there is an even spread of glue use a photographer's roller. (This will last indefinitely if it is washed under the tap immediately it has been used.)

Put 2 on 1, 3 on 2, etc., until the pile is completed. Place a strip of waxed paper against the former, then lay the laminations in place, more waxed paper and then the band saw blade. Cramp up and leave until the glue is set, first removing any surplus glue with a damp rag.

Clean off and plane down to size as soon after uncramping as possible. The glue continues to harden for some days after it is safe to handle and the harder it becomes the more blunting is the effect on the tools.

Trial and error will show that there is a limit to the curve that can be achieved by this method and a trial gluing is essential if anything like a tight curve is contemplated.

Knife cut sheets of 4 mm wood are obtainable in limited variety or strips can be sawn with a circular saw. The first method is cheaper because it is more economical, the waste in sawing is considerable. There is no reason, especially if the edges are hidden, why an expensive wood should not be backed by a cheaper one.

100a Laminating a simple curved member, showing the former, waxed paper, laminations and steel backing

100b A selection of formers used for laminating purposes. The simple one, bottom left, was used to make the back rail of the easy chair (*25*) and the others to make a chair similar to the dining chair (*78c*)

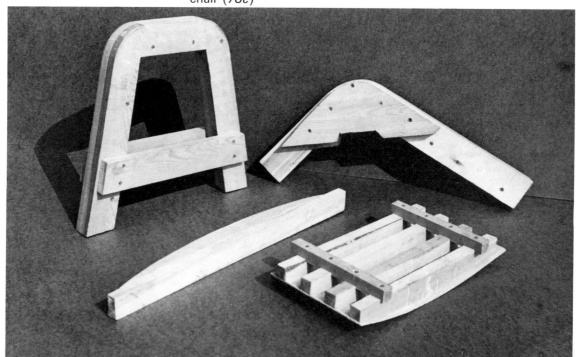

8 Materials

Dowels

Dowels are obtainable in the following diameters in 3- and 4-foot lengths.

$\frac{3}{16}$; $\frac{1}{4}$; $\frac{5}{16}$; $\frac{3}{8}$; $\frac{7}{16}$; $\frac{1}{2}$; $\frac{9}{16}$; $\frac{5}{8}$; $\frac{3}{4}$; $\frac{7}{8}$ and 1 in.

When using dowels to make a joint make at least one groove down the length to allow the surplus glue to escape out of the hole. Also round the leading edge of the dowel to make for easy entrance.

Clear sheet glass

Clear sheet glass: 18 oz $= \frac{1}{12}$ in.; 24 oz $= \frac{1}{10}$; 26 oz $= \frac{1}{8}$ in.; 32 oz $= \frac{5}{32}$ in.

Polished sheet: $\frac{3}{16}$ in. and $\frac{1}{4}$ in. thick.

Handle grips can be ground in for sliding doors.

With grooves ploughed direct into carcase make the top groove twice the depth of the bottom groove to allow for removal of glass.

Glass plates

Glass plates to suspend mirrors or hanging cabinets.

Brass with round hole: 1 in. $\times$ 22 g; $1\frac{1}{4}$ in. $\times$ 19 g; $1\frac{1}{2}$ in. $\times$ 16 g; $1\frac{3}{4}$ in. $\times$ 16 g; 2 in. $\times$ 16 g.

Brass with slotted holes: $1\frac{1}{4}$ in. $\times$ 19 g; $1\frac{1}{2}$ in. $\times$ 19 g.

Particle board (chipboard and hardboard)

Chipboard   Constructed of chips of wood which are glued and pressed to form a flat uniform board. It makes a very stable material while the movement is reduced to a minimum. It forms a very suitable base for veneers. It requires lipping for appearance sake as well as to protect the edges which are rather soft and liable to crumble. It can be obtained already veneered or covered with plastic laminate.

Standard sizes   8, 9, 10, 12, 16, 17 $\times$ 4 and 16, 17 $\times$ 5 (in feet) and 9, 12, 15, 18, 22 mm thick.

Veneered sheets 8 $\times$ 4 and 12 or 18 mm thick.

Hardboard   Made from raw wood which has been processed.

Standard thickness $\frac{1}{8}$ in. or $\frac{3}{16}$ in.

Sheets 6, 8, 9, 10, 12 × 4; 8 × 5; 6 × 2; $6\frac{1}{2}$ × $2\frac{1}{2}$ (in feet).

Oiled   Has greater density, strength and hardness.

Perforated with $\frac{3}{16}$ in. holes at $\frac{1}{2}$ in. or $\frac{3}{4}$ in. centres.

Sheets 6 or 9 × 4 ft, thickness $\frac{1}{8}$ in.

Finishes   Various, reeded, leather grained, etc., and covered with decorative laminate or stove enamelled.

Plywood

Plywood is made up of sheets of veneer glued with alternate veneers laid up at right angles to each other. This distributes the longitudinal strength of the wood in all directions. The small movement of the board is much less than that of solid timber and a greater stability is obtained (*101a*).

It varies in the species of veneer used, its grade, thickness, type of adhesive, size of sheet and surface finish. A great variety of plywood is obtainable with many different woods. It is possible to have a decorative veneer on one side and a plain one on the other or to have both sides decorative or the plywood can be made of all the same timber, e.g. birch. Plywood is graded according to the quality of the veneers and adhesive which are used and these vary with the country of origin.

As an example the following details apply to *Finnish-Birch plywood:*
Grading

   A   Practically free from all defects.
   B   Some small pin knots, joints glued and matched, slight discoloration allowable.
   S   Good painting quality, knots, joints glued, discoloration allowed.
 BB   Knots plugged, joints and discoloration.
WG   All defects allowed; only guaranteed well glued.

(Plugs exist where knots have been stamped out and filled and show as elliptical shapes.)

One side B and the other BB is quite a usual grading.

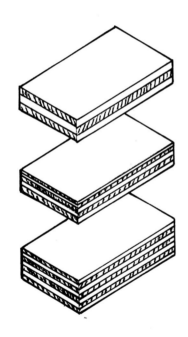

101a Three ply
      Five ply
      Multiply

Glues   Casein, Blood Albumen, Extended Resin and W.B.P. are used.

Sizes of sheet   Thickness from 3 to 24 mm.

In inches
38 × 38; 42 × 42; 50/60 × 50/60/72/84/96/108/120/132/138/144; 72 × 50/60; 84 × 50.

Qualities   A/BB; B/BB; B/WG; S/BB; S/WG; BB; BB/WG; WG.

Strips 1 in. wide are placed together with or without glue between outer veneers with the grain direction at right angles to the grain core (*101b*).

Finnish Birch blockboard

Core wood   Pine, Spruce or Fir.

Thickness   16, 18, 19, 22 and 25 mm.

Glue   Extended resin.

Sizes in in.   50 × 72/84/96/120/144; 60 × 72/84/96/120/144.

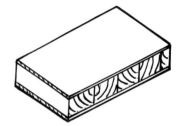

101b Blockboard
Core made up on strips
up to 1 in. wide with or
without glue between

Strips of wood which vary from 15 to 7 mm glued together face to face between outer veneers. This is more expensive and heavier (due to glue weight) than blockboard but more stable (*101c*).

Finnish Birch laminboard

Core wood   Pine or Birch.

Thickness   16, 18, 19, 22 and 25 mm.

Glue   Extended resin.

Sizes in in.   50 × 72/84/96/120/144; 60 × 72/84/96/120/144.

Both blockboard and laminboard make a firm stable base on which to veneer but both require lipping.

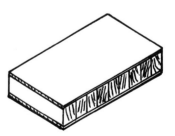

101c Laminboard
Core made up of strips
between 1·5 and 7 mm
wide glued together

Protective covering (laminated plastic, vinyl and felt)

Thermoset plastic (or laminated plastic)

These can be obtained in a variety of colours and designs with either a high gloss or a semi-matt finish, in sheets $\frac{1}{16}$ in. thick. This is a very hard wearing material and will withstand normal heat and is reasonably scratch proof and entirely resistant to water. It is usually secured with an impact adhesive to its foundation. It can be purchased already bonded to hardboard or chipboard.

Standard sizes $10 \times 4; 9 \times 4; 8 \times 4; 10 \times 3; 8 \times 3; 10 \times 2\frac{1}{2}; 8 \times 2\frac{1}{2}$ (in feet).

Self adhesive vinyl

This makes a very useful material for shelf lining or tray bottom covering. It can be bought in a variety of colours and designs. The backing is removed and the sheet will adhere securely, requiring only a wipe with a damp cloth to keep it clean.

Standard sizes   Sold by the yard either 18 in. or 36 in. wide.

Self adhesive felt

Obtainable either red or green. This is excellent for putting on the underside of bowls or table lamps, etc.

Standard sizes   Sold by the yard either $16\frac{1}{2}$ or 33 in. wide.

Screws

Table of gauges available up to 10. Preferred sizes only

Length	Steel wood screws Countersunk heads	Brass wood screws Countersunk heads	Brass wood screws Round head
$\frac{1}{4}$ in.		1, 2	
$\frac{3}{8}$ in.	2–4	1–4	2–4
$\frac{1}{2}$ in.	2–8	2–6	2–6
$\frac{5}{8}$ in.	3–8	3–6	4–6
$\frac{3}{4}$ in.	4–10	4–8	4–8
$\frac{7}{8}$ in.	6–8		
1 in.	4–10	4–10	4–8, 10
$1\frac{1}{4}$ in.	6–10	6–10	6, 8, 10
$1\frac{1}{2}$ in.	6–10	6, 8–10	8, 10
$1\frac{3}{4}$ in.	8–10	10	
2 in.	6, 8–10	8, 10	
$2\frac{1}{4}$ in.	10		
3 in.	8, 10		

Mirror screw

Chromium plated brass countersunk head screws with chromium plated, polished brass dome tops.

$\frac{3}{4}$ in. by 8; 1 in. by 8, 10; $1\frac{1}{4}$ in. by 8, 10; $1\frac{1}{2}$ in. by 8, 10; 2 in by 8, 10.

Skiver

For bureau falls.

Smooth grained sheepskin, various colours.
Skins 6 to 10 square feet.

Dryad Handicrafts, Northgates, Leicester.

Upholstery materials and fittings

Foam   Various types of latex and plastic foam and practically any size is obtainable.

B & M (Latex) Sales Ltd, 35 Station Road, Addlestone, Surrey, will supply and advise.

Pass plates metal   These are $19\frac{1}{2}$ in. long with 9 spring holes and can be cut to a smaller size if required.

Springs, plastic covered tension   Obtainable in lengths 14 to 22 by inches. Add $1\frac{1}{2}$ in. for stretched length.

Webbing   Bonded fabric and rubber.
In widths of $\frac{3}{4}$ in.; $1\frac{1}{8}$ in.; $1\frac{1}{2}$ in.; 2 in.; $2\frac{1}{4}$ in.

Carpet fasteners   These consist of a screw to take a snap fastener and are useful to hold loose upholstery in position.

Vinyl   There are on the market a wide range of vinyl materials which are fist class for dining chair seats and other upholstery purposes. They are very hard wearing and can be easily cleaned. They are flexible, do not crack and can be obtained in different textures and a variety of colours. They will outlast most of the more conventional materials.

Commercial Plastics Ltd, Berkeley Square House, Berkeley Square, London W1.

9 Fittings

Bolts

102 Stamped brass barrel bolts. $\frac{7}{8}$ in. wide with $\frac{1}{4}$ in. shoot. 2 in. and 3 in. long

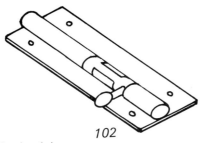

102

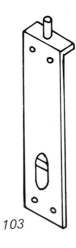

103 Brass flush bolts. 3 in. by $\frac{1}{2}$ in.

103

Castors

104 Heavy duty castors. Nylon socket requiring $\frac{1}{2}$ in. D hole $1\frac{3}{4}$ in. deep. Wheels, black plastic, moulded nylon or off-white rubber tyred $1\frac{5}{8}$ in. or 2 in. wheels

105 Plain trolley castors. Off-white rubber tyres. Steel socket requiring $\frac{3}{8}$ in. D hole $1\frac{3}{4}$ in. deep

106 Ball type castor. Either plate mounting as illustrated or socket type. Plate $1\frac{3}{4}$ in. square with 4 screw holes. Nylon socket requiring $\frac{1}{2}$ in. D hole $1\frac{3}{4}$ in. deep

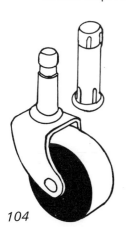

104

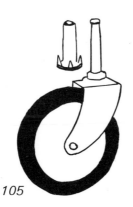

105

106

Catches

107   Ball catches—brass. Diameter of barrel $\frac{3}{16}$ in.; $\frac{1}{4}$ in.; $\frac{5}{16}$ in.; $\frac{3}{8}$ in.; $\frac{1}{2}$ in.; $\frac{5}{8}$ in.
Roller catch—nylon. As above with nylon instead of brass and nylon roller in place of steel ball. $\frac{3}{4}$ in. barrel

108   Brass catch as illustrated. Gripped by two steel balls adjustable for pressure. $1\frac{15}{16}$ in. long

109   Nylon catches. Available in many slightly different forms

110, 111   Magnetic catches. Various patterns, some with the magnets enclosed in plastic, others in brass

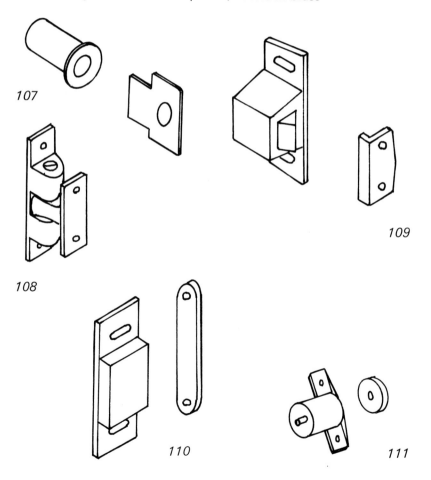

107

108

109

110

111

Hinges

112 Brass butt pressed steel pin. 1 in. $\times$ $\frac{1}{2}$ in.; $1\frac{1}{4}$ in. $\times$ $\frac{5}{8}$ in.; $1\frac{1}{2}$ in. $\times$ $\frac{3}{4}$ in.; 2 in. $\times$ 1 in.; $2\frac{1}{2}$ in. $\times$ $1\frac{1}{4}$ in.; 3 in. $\times$ $1\frac{1}{2}$ in.

113 Brass butt broad suite solid machine iron or brass pin. $1\frac{1}{2}$ in. $\times$ $\frac{7}{8}$ in.; $1\frac{3}{4}$ in. $\times$ 1 in.; 2 in. $\times$ $1\frac{1}{8}$ in.; $2\frac{1}{2}$ in. $\times$ $1\frac{3}{8}$ in.; 3 in. $\times$ $1\frac{5}{8}$ in.

114 Brass butt narrow suite solid machine iron or brass pin. 1 in. $\times$ $\frac{5}{8}$ in.; $1\frac{1}{4}$ in. $\times$ $\frac{11}{16}$ in.; $1\frac{1}{2}$ in. $\times$ $\frac{3}{4}$ in.

115 Brass back flap solid machine steel pin. 1 in. $\times$ $1\frac{5}{8}$ in.; $1\frac{1}{4}$ in. $\times$ $1\frac{7}{8}$ in.; $1\frac{1}{2}$ in. $\times$ $2\frac{3}{8}$ in.

116 Continuous hinge brass. Widths open 1 in.; $1\frac{1}{4}$ in.; $1\frac{1}{2}$ in. Available any length up to 6 ft with holes at 2 in. centre or without holes

117 Brass cranked kitchen cabinet hinge. Also supplied un-cranked. $1\frac{1}{2}$ in. for either $\frac{3}{8}$ in. or $\frac{1}{4}$ in. wood

118 Brass strap or desk hinge. First measurement length of strap, second width. 1 in. $\times$ $\frac{5}{16}$ in.; $1\frac{1}{4}$ in. $\times$ $\frac{3}{8}$ in.; $1\frac{1}{2}$ in. $\times$ $\frac{1}{2}$ in.; 2 in. $\times$ $\frac{1}{2}$ in.; $2\frac{1}{4}$ in. $\times$ $\frac{5}{8}$ in.

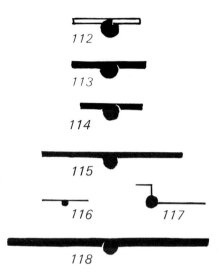

112

113

114

115

116   117

118

Lamp fittings

119 Threaded to fit lamp holder at top
Coarse thread to grip in wood at bottom

120 Threaded at top to fit lamp holder
Held in place by screws

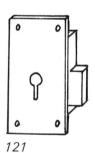

119   120

121

Locks

121 Straight brass double hand lock
Brass cap 2 levers
2 in. and 3 in.

122 Drawer locks
Brass cap 2 levers
2 in. and $2\frac{1}{2}$ in.

123 Chest locks
Brass cap 2 levers
2 in. and $2\frac{1}{2}$ in.

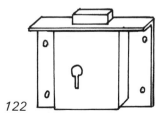
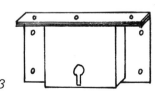

122   123

Stays

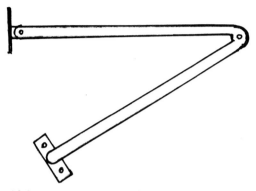

124 Bureau and desk stays
Brass, left or right hand
Sizes closed 3 in.; 4 in.; 5 in.; 6 in.

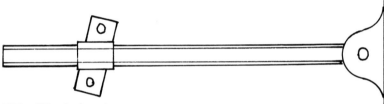

125 Wardrobe stays
Brass with nylon slide
Length overall $8\frac{1}{2}$ in.

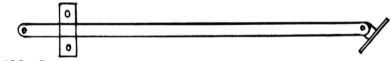

126 Brass
Length overall $7\frac{1}{2}$ in.; $10\frac{1}{2}$ in.

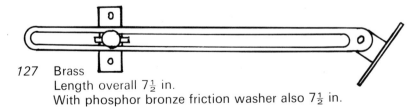

127 Brass
Length overall $7\frac{1}{2}$ in.
With phosphor bronze friction washer also $7\frac{1}{2}$ in.

Sliding doors

128   Fibre channel
Black plastic for $\frac{1}{4}$ in. plate glass
Single channel
      Bottom section $\frac{13}{32}$ × $\frac{3}{8}$ in., depth of groove $\frac{1}{4}$ in.
      Top section $\frac{13}{32}$ × $\frac{1}{2}$ in., depth of groove $\frac{3}{8}$ in.
Double channel
      Bottom section $\frac{25}{32}$ × $\frac{3}{8}$ in., depth of groove $\frac{1}{4}$ in.
      Top section $\frac{25}{32}$ × $\frac{1}{2}$ in., depth of groove $\frac{3}{8}$ in.
Both obtainable in 6 ft and 7 ft lengths

129   Fibre track
Inserted type   A $\frac{1}{2}$ in. high × $\frac{5}{32}$ in. wide
                  B $\frac{9}{16}$ in. high × $\frac{7}{32}$ in. wide

130   Surface type   C $\frac{7}{16}$ in. base × $\frac{1}{4}$ in.
                      D $\frac{1}{2}$ in. base × $\frac{5}{16}$ in.
Both obtainable in 6 ft to 6 ft 6 in. lengths

131   Fibre slides to run along track
      E $\frac{13}{16}$ in. × $\frac{11}{32}$ in. × $\frac{3}{8}$ in. high
      F $2\frac{3}{8}$ in. × $\frac{7}{16}$ in. × $\frac{1}{2}$ in. high

128

129

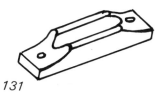

130

131

10 Glues

There are many different adhesives on the market and it is essential that the right choice is made. It is no good expecting·a satisfactory joint to be made with the wrong glue. A glue which will give an excellent bond between wood and wood will not necessarily be effective for other materials.

The furniture maker is mainly concerned with wood to wood and so glues that are suitable for that purpose are most fully dealt with. These glues can be classified according to certain factors. The craftsman wants, ideally, a glue that allows him plenty of time to assemble and adjust his work; will then set quickly so that he can start cleaning up; will not stain; is durable; will last a long time on the shelf; a glue that while not exactly 'gap' filling will at least make up the normal space left in a joint. The various types of glue which are available are dealt with separately and then a table of these wood to wood glues is given to summarise their advantages and disadvantages.

The process of gluing takes place in three stages. The first stage is the period allowed for adjustment before everything must be in its final position with cramps tight and frames square. This is called the gelling time and it must be long enough to allow the essential adjustments to be made. The second is the time for which the cramps must be left on and before any more work can be done. The last period is that which must elapse before full strength has developed.

Glues have been evolved which are practically indestructible by micro-organisms, damp, wet, heat and physical stress. If two boards are carefully glued edge to edge, with one of these glues, and an attempt made to break the joint it will be found that the wood fractures not the glue.

With the modern adhesives it is essential that the manufacturer's instructions are faithfully followed. Most of these have a technical service and will be only too willing to help and advise.

Scotch glue

This has been largely superseded by more efficient glues, except for hand veneering. Its disadvantage is that it requires heating to prepare and must also be applied hot. When it has to be kept hot for a long time it tends to become too thick and should it boil its strength is dangerously reduced. In a cold workshop it is liable to chill too quickly and gell before the joint is properly together. It is not waterproof and requires longer in cramps than most modern adhesives.

It is useful for veneering because it has tack, that is it has a certain amount of immediate grip; it can also be softened by heating through the veneer with a hot iron over a damp cloth. (This overcomes the problem of gelling when veneering a large surface.)

There have been developed cold setting animal glues which are very useful for gluing in bands and strings. They have a much longer working time than ordinary hot glue. They remain liquid at normal temperatures experienced during the summer but in winter it may be necessary to stand the tin in warm water to make it fluid.

Resin glues

The group of glues which come under the heading of urea-formaldehyde provide a very strong bond which is almost in-destructible. It is put out in two forms, two part and single application.

Two part application   Here the adhesive comes in two parts, a hardener which is a colourless liquid and a white powder. The hardener is ready for use but the powder requires dissolving in water. The powder should be added to the water. It is advisable to allow some hours between mixing and using so that all the air bubbles which develop during mixing have time to disperse. Once the solution, which should be of a syrupy consistency, has been made it will last for at least a month.

The glue and the hardener are applied separately. In the case of a mortise and tenon the easiest method is to apply the hardener to the tenon, using a stick to which has been tied a piece of rag. (Do not use a brush with any metal because this will cause staining.) The glue is put in the mortise hole with a stick. Keep the two containers well away from each other because it will only take a drop of hardener in the glue to set it and render it useless.

All the joints have the glue and hardener applied before any are put together. Since no reaction takes place until contact, the gelling time does not start until then. This allows a much longer time for a complicated assembly. (The hardener-coated surface must still be damp when the two halves of the joints are finally brought together.)

The work will require cramping until the glue is set. The cramps should not be so tight that they exclude all the glue. The gelling and setting time can be controlled by the temperature of the room and the hardener used. The manufacturers supply a table showing the effect of temperature on these times and the variety of hardener available.

The average working time is 15 minutes and it can be un-cramped in 3 hours, even though full strength has not yet been achieved. It is an advantage to remove any surplus glue while it is still fluid. The longer it is left the harder it becomes and the more blunting the effect will be on the tools.

To prevent any staining resulting from the glue, the iron of the cramp and the wood itself coming into contact, it is advisable to insert a piece of paper between the cramp and the glue where this could occur.

Single application   This same type of glue can be purchased as a powder to be dissolved in water and applied as a single operation. The hardener, in dehydrated form, being already present in the glue powder. This will have a limited life and only sufficient for immediate application should be mixed. It will not allow for the same manoeuvering time as the separate application glue because 'gelling' will start once the glue is mixed with water.

While temperature does affect the setting time the glue is cold setting. A hot workshop will shorten the setting time and a cold one lengthen it.

P.V.A.

This stands for polyvinyl acetate and is a thermoplastic glue. This means that after it sets it can be softened by heating. Since furniture will not normally be subjected to temperature increases of this order this does not make it in any way an unsuitable furniture glue.

It is supplied ready for use, requiring no heating or mixing, as a white liquid. It is applied to one half of the joint only and is clean and easy to use. This makes it an extremely useful adhesive for a school or home workshop.

The joint will require cramping although some tack will be experienced. The setting time is down to about an hour depending upon local conditions. The glue itself is liable to stain some woods and for this reason must be used carefully.

Casein glue

This is a glue made from curds derived from filtering off the whey from skimmed milk and treating it with chemicals. This is another white powder which requires mixing with water. It is a single application glue and requires cramping. It will stain some woods with a high tannin content, e.g. oak. Only sufficient glue for immediate use should be mixed. It sets by chemical action and evaporation of water. After mixing allow 20 minutes for the powder to dissolve (add powder to water).

Epoxy resin

These glues do not produce volatile components and so can be used between non-porous surfaces, i.e. metal to metal. As with all glues it is essential that the two surfaces to be joined are perfectly clean. It is equally suitable for joining wood and metal. It is supplied in two tubes, one of glue and the other hardener. A sufficient quantity for immediate use is squeezed out and mixed in equal proportions from each tube.

Impact adhesive

This is a synthetic rubber and resin glue especially designed for gluing laminated plastic sheeting to wood. All surfaces should be clean and slightly roughened. The glue is applied to both surfaces and allowed to dry for 10 to 15 minutes. If they are then brought into contact with hand pressure they will immediately knit together. Although full strength is not developed for 48 hours the work can be handled immediately.

Great care must be taken to ensure that the laminate goes into its correct position because re-adjustment will not be possible. When surfacing a table top or other large area some means must be found of making a stop or ledge along the far edge so that the sheet can be lowered into position pressed against it. This can be done by cramping a lath along it or by drawing pins placed so that their edges stick above the level of the top.

Latex and resin

Particularly useful for upholstery work, being strong and clean to use. Comes ready for use as a white liquid. Braid, for example, which used to be fastened with gimp pins can now be held in place with glue.

Makes and types of glues

	Scotch	Resin	P.V.A.	Casein	Impact	Latex	Epoxy
Bardens (Bury) Ltd, Hollins Vale Works, Bury, Lancs.	Calabar	—	—	—	—	—	—
Bostik Ltd, Leicester	—	—	Bostik Bond P.V.A.	—	Bostik Contact 3	—	Bostik 7
CIBA(ARL), Duxford, Cambridge	—	Aerolite 306	—	—	—	—	Araldite
Croid Ltd, Imperial House, Kingsway, London W.C.2	Aero	—	Polystik	—	—	Fabrex	—
Evo-Stik, Evode Ltd, 450/2 Edgware Road, London W.2	—	—	Resin W	—	Evo-Stik Impact	—	—
Leicester, Lovell & Co. Ltd, North Baddesley, Southampton	—	Cascamite One Shot	Casco P.V.A.	Casco	—	—	—

This only shows certain manufacturers; there may well be others making glues equally efficient.

Comparative table of glues

	Useful life Unmixed	Mixed	Gelling Time	Setting Time	Full Strength	Staining	Durability	Preparation
Casein	1 year	5 hours		2–4 hours	12 hours	Slight	Interior	Mixed cold
P.V.A.	1 year		15 mins	1 hour	20 hours	Slight	Interior	Ready mixed
Resin Separate Hardener	2 years	2 months	15 mins	3 hours	48 hours	In contact with metal	Moisture resistant	Mixed cold
Resin Combined Hardener	1 year	1–3 hours	20 mins	2–4 hours	48 hours	In contact with metal	Moisture resistant	Mixed cold
Scotch Hot	Unlimited		5–10 mins	12 hours	48 hours	Nil	Interior	Mixed hot
Scotch Cold	Unlimited		20 mins	2 hours	48 hours	Nil	Interior	Ready

All the times quoted above should be taken as only a rough guide because local conditions will be the deciding factor.
The Durability Grades are those assigned to the particular types of glue by the Forest Products Research.

The information in this section comes from manufacturer's technical sheets and the following booklets:

Forest Products Research, Bulletin No. 20, *Requirements and Properties of Adhesives for Wood*, H.M.S.O. Department of Scientific and Industrial Research.

Timber Research and Development Association, Construction Research, Bulletin No. 2, *Glues and Their Uses*.

Gluing up

The notes are intended as reminders because this is such a vital stage. A lot of good work is spoilt through a lack of attention to essential detail and a failure to allow sufficient time.

Using a simple frame as an example

1   Assemble the work 'dry', that is without glue. If the joints do not fit then the addition of glue will not correct this.

2(a)   Test for squareness by comparing the diagonals. This can be done with a lath sharpened to a flat point at one end. If both diagonals measure the same then the frame is square. If not, move the diagonals in the direction of the long diagonal until they are (*132a* and *b*).

(b)   Sight the frame carefully in the direction indicated by the arrow to see if it is 'out of wind' (*133c* shows a frame in wind). Raise the low corners by slacking the cramps and lifting them until the front and back rails are in line. When this happens they are out of wind. Should the frame be badly out and resist this correction it means that one or more mortise holes or tenons are out of true and these must be corrected.

3   Uncramp, clean up and polish the inside faces.

4   Glue up following the procedure outlined in 2(a) and (b).

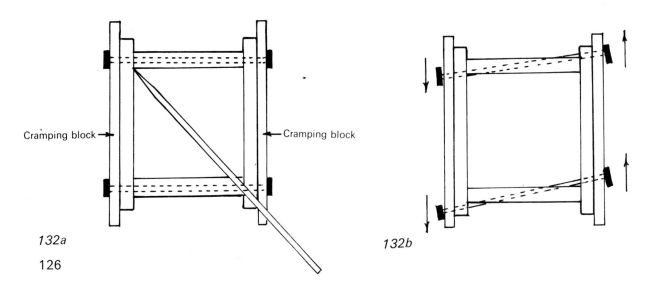

Cramping block →   ← Cramping block

132a

132b

Gluing up a stool

This is a more difficult proposition and must be glued in stages rather than all at once.

1   Each of the four frames must be cramped up dry as indicated in 2(a) and (b) for the simple frame.

2   Two opposite frames are cleaned up and glued. In *133a* that is either frames A and C or D and B.

3   When these are ready the complete stool can be cramped up for the first time. Using *133a*, assuming that frames A and C are already glued, the diagonals of D and B must now be checked.

4   The diagonals of the top and bottom must next be tested proceeding as shown in *133d*.

5   The final gluing can take place followed immediately by the tests which were made during the preliminary check.

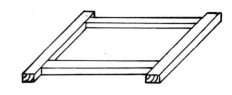

133b

133c

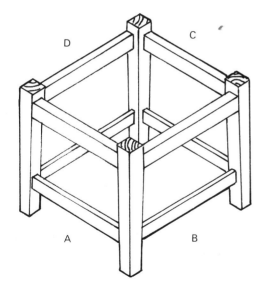

133a

133d

Cramping blocks

The work should always be protected from the face of the cramps. This is done by using a piece of soft wood. This has the added function of spreading the pressure of the cramp over a much wider area. In the case of the frame mentioned earlier they should stretch the full length of the frame. These are shown in *132a* and *b*.

It may sometimes be necessary to shape the blocks when gluing an assembly where the angles are not right angles. An example of this is a coffee table with splayed legs. When the legs and rails are glued, in order to cramp them up, shaped blocks are introduced (see *134a*). If the angle is at all great the blocks will slide as soon as pressure is applied. If this happens they should themselves be glued on to the legs before the actual gluing takes place. They can be easily removed when they are no longer required by sawing and planing.

When gluing a shelf into a wide carcase it is sometimes difficult to get the necessary pressure in the middle. This can be achieved by curving the cramping block so that the pressure is first applied in the middle and then at the edges as the block is straightened out with the force of the cramp. This is illustrated in *134b*. This problem does not occur at the top or bottom because 3 or even 4 cramps can be introduced here if necessary.

The faces of all the cramping blocks which come into contact with the piece being glued must be planed and smooth. If this is not done they will leave dents and marks behind.

Dovetails

The easiest way to glue up dovetails is to leave $\frac{1}{32}$ in. on the thickness of the wood bearing the tails when planing up. Gauge to thickness in the usual way but stop $\frac{1}{32}$ in. before reaching this gauge line. If this is done a cramping block can be put straight across the joint (*134c*), because the tails stand proud.

Polish

It is best to exclude all polish from the joints but it is absolutely essential that any wax should be kept out. If this is not done there will be a failure of that joint.

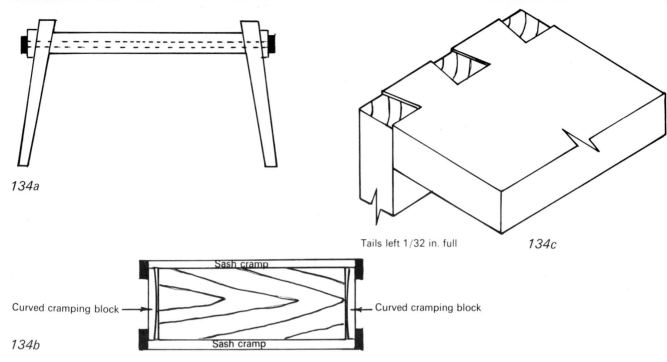

134a

134c

Tails left 1/32 in. full

134b

Sash cramp

Curved cramping block →   ← Curved cramping block

Sash cramp

135

11 Wood finishing

Preparing for polish

As much cleaning up as possible should be done with a smoothing plane which is sharp, has its mouth and cap iron set close and is finely set. This gives a very clean finish and is economical of time. A more difficult piece of wood with contrary grain may require a cabinet scraper but this should be used with caution to avoid making hollows which will show when the final polish is applied.

Follow this up with 'O' glasspaper and then 'Flour' grade, wrapped round a cork block. It must be realised that the success or otherwise of the finish is being laid down now. The polish will not disguise or hide any imperfections but only exaggerate and make them more obvious. The glasspaper must be used with the grain or the result, even with these fine grades, will be a series of scratches across the grain.

When woods are dampened there is a tendency for the grain to lift and this occurs with some polishes. This can be minimised by damping the surface, causing the grain to rise and then glass-papering again. This will ensure a smooth surface.

If the surface has been dented this can be corrected with a damp cloth and iron. Place a damp cloth over the mark and apply a hot iron. Provided that it is just a dent and no wood has been removed the steam will draw it up. Continue until the wood is slightly higher than the rest and then glasspaper it down.

Most of the dents which are discovered are due to a lack of thought during making. Each time a piece of wood is put down on the bench the surface of the bench should be cleared otherwise there will be small chips of wood trapped between the wood and the bench top and these will cause dents to form.

All polishing should be done in as near a dust free atmosphere as possible. This is particularly important with the harder finishes where the dust particles will form little blebs all over the surface.

Wax polish

There is no polish which leaves the wood as near its natural colour and which improves with the passage of time, like a good wax polish. Unfortunately it is not very durable and is spoilt with a drop of water or spirit (although this damage is repairable) and is inclined to show finger marks and has no resistance to abrasion.

All these defects would seem to rule it out as a finish but this would be wrong. It is admirable for such purposes as dining room chairs, the underframing of tables, bureaux and bookcases but unsuitable for table tops or uncovered dressing-table tops.

It has the great virtue that it is very easy to apply. First prepare the surface of the wood. Now brush on a coat of bleached shellac which has been diluted with 50 per cent methylated spirit. (It will be found to be too thick for this purpose undiluted.) This is done to fill the grain and prepare the wood for the wax. When the polish is dry, and this can be speeded up by rubbing it in with the ball of the hand, remove any polish left on the surface of the wood with flour paper. This should leave the surface perfectly smooth and shiny. A very absorbent wood may require two coats. The glasspaper is used without a block and as soon as it clogs a fresh part must be used or it will scratch the wood. The wax is now applied sparingly with a stiff cloth and left a little while for the solvent to evaporate and then polished. Several coats may be necessary and at the end the wood should gleam and show itself to full advantage.

The wax can be made by dissolving beeswax in turpentine but a proprietary brand of chilled wax gives a more lasting and harder polish. The beeswax will also give a yellow tinge, but the chilled wax can be obtained much lighter in colour and avoids this effect. As the finished article is regularly polished it will build up a most attractive shine.

Chilled wax

J. Nicholson & Sons,
Longlands Works,
Windermere

If a wax polished surface is damaged, by water for example, the old wax can be removed by rubbing with very fine wire wool and turpentine and then re-polished. If it is only a small mark a piece of flour paper charged with wax polish will usually suffice.

Polyurethane varnish

There are a number of these varnishes on the market which are available in small quantities. The first coat can be applied with a cloth or brush. Care should be taken to 'float' the coat on, and any attempt to brush it out like a paint will spoil the finish. Watch the edges carefully so as to avoid tears.

When this coat is dry it should be flatted down with either flour paper or a very fine wire wool. This will remove any of the little blebs which may have formed and which would spoil the finished surface.

The second coat, which is best applied with a brush, should not be started until the first coat is hard, which will take about six hours depending on the temperature. A thin even coat should be put on, again watching the edges carefully.

Two coats are sufficient for most purposes but a third one can be added if desired. If the wood has a very open grain it may be necessary to use the first coat as a filler and rub it right down and then apply the normal two coats. The resulting finish is very hard wearing and is resistant to water, heat and spirit. It will keep its gloss and only require a wipe with a damp cloth to keep it clean.

Catalyst lacquer

To achieve the maximum protection of the wood it is necessary to use one of the catalyst lacquers or plastic coatings, or cold catalyst polishes. These names used by different manufacturers make for some confusion.

They consist of a mixture of three parts, a resin, a catalyst and an accelerator. The accelerator is to enable the reaction to take place at normal temperatures and without the catalyst nothing would happen at all. In most cases the accelerator has already been added to the resin and it only requires the addition of the catalyst to make it ready for use. The resulting mix varies with different makes but most will remain in a usable condition overnight.

The first coat should be diluted with thinners to act as a grain filler. The second one, full strength, can be brushed on as soon as this is dry. When this also has had time to dry rub over the surface lightly with a fine grade of wet and dry paper (used wet) to denib (that is remove any blebs that have appeared). The final coat can now be put on. Leave this overnight to harden.

The degree of gloss depends upon the amount of work that is done at this last stage. First of all rub down with fine wet and dry paper, again used wet, and follow this up with a burnishing cream. As the work proceeds the gloss will appear and as soon as it is satisfactory it can stop. The polish is practically indestructible under normal conditions and has a high resistance to abrasion.

With an article like a coffee table it is useful to use this finish for the top and to polish the underframing with wax.

Read the manufacturer's instructions carefully before starting.

Polyurethane varnish

Ronseal   Izal Ltd,
           Thorncliffe,
           Sheffield, S30 4YP

Plastic coating
(Complete with thinners
and burnishing cream)

Rustins   Rustins Ltd,
           Waterloo Road,
           London, N.W.2

Bourne seal

This is a most efficient wood seal and is mentioned by name because there does not seem to be another equivalent product on the market. It is recommended for table tops and similar surfaces which are liable to experience hard wear and have water and other liquids spilt on them. It is also reasonably heat proof.

The first coat is floated on with a rag and allowed to dry overnight. The surface should be lightly rubbed down with flour paper to remove any blebs. Carefully dust the surface and apply the second coat with a brush with light easy strokes, only brushing enough to ensure an even flow.

Teak oil

For those who require an oiled finish teak oil is the answer and it is very easy to apply with a cloth and does not darken the wood unduly. Apply one coat and after a few minutes remove any surplus oil. When this coat is dry in about six hours, put on another coat in the same way.

Other items

Fillers, plastic wood and stains are best avoided. The former will show through natural finishes, the second is used only to fill holes which should not be there and is immediately obvious and if you select the right wood then stain is unnecessary.

Abrasive materials

Glass paper   Preferably of the dark glass variety which is recommended for uniformity of cut. Grades 00, 0, 1, $1\frac{1}{2}$, F2, M2, S2, $2\frac{1}{2}$, 3.

Garnet paper   Close or open coat, the latter being better for soft or resinous wood. Grades 5/0, 4/0, 3/0, 2/0, 1/0, $\frac{1}{2}$, 1, $1\frac{1}{2}$, 2. (These are arranged to correspond with the glass paper grades, i.e., 5/0 is equivalent to 00, etc.)

Waterproof carborundum (Wet and Dry paper)   Used with water and having a back proof against water, petrol, oil and alcohol. Grades 400, 320, 280, 240, 220, 180, 150. (The finest grade comes first.)

Lubrisil   Non-clogging. Grades 400, 320, etc., as for Waterproof carborundum.

Bourne seal

Floor Treatments Ltd,
Lloyds Bank Chambers,
High Street,
High Wycombe,
Bucks.

12 Useful sizes

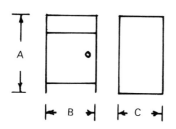

Bedside cabinet

	in.	mm
A	27–30	686–762
B	14–16	356–406
C	13–15	330–381

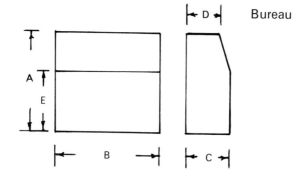

Bureau

	in.	mm
A	38–40	965–1016
B	24–36	610–914
C	16–18	406–457
D	8–10	203–254
E	30	762

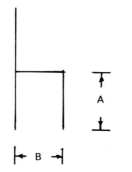

Chair

	in.	mm
A	18–19	457–483
B	14–16	356–406

	in.	mm
A	24	610
B	18	457

Fire screen

	in.	mm
A	21–22	533–559
B	17	432
C	12	305

Piano stool

	in.	mm
A	11	279

Stool

	in.	mm
A	60	1524

Standard lamp

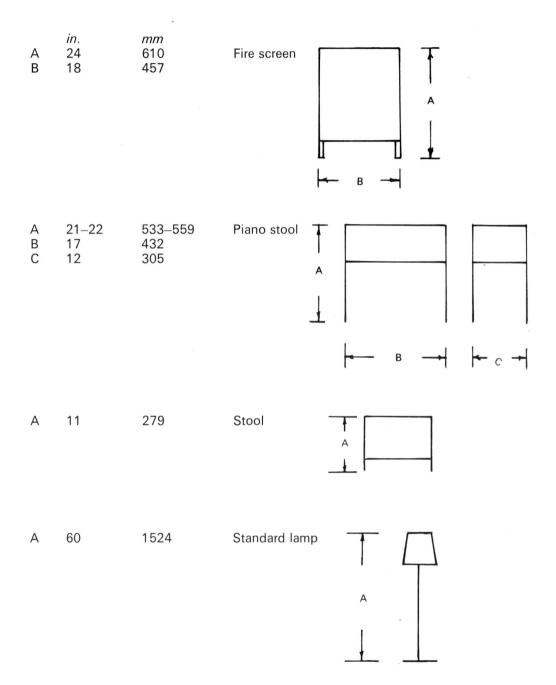

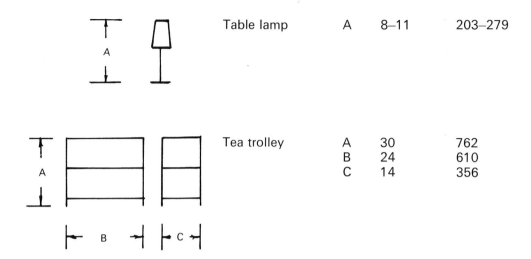

Table lamp	A	8–11	203–279

Tea trolley	A	30	762
	B	24	610
	C	14	356

Suitable sizes for common articles

		in.	mm
Books	Large	15 × 12	381 × 305
	Medium	8½ × 5½	216 × 140
	Small	7 × 4½	178 × 114
Crockery	Dinner plate	11	279
	Tea plate	7	178
	Saucer	6	152
	Cup	3	76
Cutlery	Large knife	9½	241
	Small knife	8	203
	Large spoon	8	203
	Small spoon	6½	165
	Teaspoon	5	127
	Carving knife	13	330
Letters	Large	9 × 4	229 × 102
	Regular	6 × 3¾	152 × 95
Magazines		13½ × 11	343 × 279
Milk bottle		9 × 3	229 × 76
Music		13 × 10	330 × 254
Paper	Foolscap	13 × 8	330 × 203
	Quarto	10½ × 8	267 × 203
Pencil		7	178
Records	L.P.	12½ × 12½	318 × 318
	E.P.	6½ × 7½	165 × 191

Conversion table from inches to millimetres

1 in. = 25·4 mm

Decimals of an inch	in.	mm	in.	mm	ft	mm
0·0312	$\frac{1}{32}$	0·79	1	25	1	305
0·0625	$\frac{1}{16}$	1·59	2	51	2	610
0·125	$\frac{1}{8}$	3·18	3	76	3	914
0·1875	$\frac{3}{16}$	4·76	4	102	4	1219
0·25	$\frac{1}{4}$	6·35	5	127	5	1524
0·3125	$\frac{5}{16}$	7·94	6	152	6	1829
0·375	$\frac{3}{8}$	9·53	7	178		
0·4375	$\frac{7}{16}$	11·11	8	203		
0·5	$\frac{1}{2}$	12·70	9	229		
0·5625	$\frac{9}{16}$	14·29	10	254		
0·625	$\frac{5}{8}$	15·88	11	279		
0·6875	$\frac{11}{16}$	17·46	12	305		
0·75	$\frac{3}{4}$	19·05				
0·8125	$\frac{13}{16}$	20·64				
0·875	$\frac{7}{8}$	22·23				
0·9375	$\frac{15}{16}$	23·81				
	1	25·4				

All metric measurements are quoted in millimetres although no firm decision on the unit to be eventually used has yet been made.

Index